William Shepard Walsh

**Pen Pictures of modern Authors**

William Shepard Walsh

**Pen Pictures of modern Authors**

ISBN/EAN: 9783743332171

Manufactured in Europe, USA, Canada, Australia, Japa

Cover: Foto ©ninafisch / pixelio.de

Manufactured and distributed by brebook publishing software (www.brebook.com)

William Shepard Walsh

**Pen Pictures of modern Authors**

THE LITERARY LIFE

*Edited by*
*WILLIAM SHEPARD*

*Pen Pictures of Modern Authors*

NEW YORK
G. P. PUTNAM'S SONS
27 AND 29 WEST 23D STREET
1882

*Press of
G. P. Putnam's Sons
New York*

## PREFACE.

THESE are not biographies that are collected here, but a series of sketches, anecdotes, and personal reminiscences relating to the more modern authors—that is, the authors who are now living, or who have died very recently and whose work belongs to the present half of the century. As the book is a compilation, the editor has occasionally been hampered by want of available material, and if the reader misses any face which he would like to have seen in a gallery of this sort, he will understand that it is because no satisfactory "pen picture" could be found.

The thanks of the editor are due to the publishers of the various magazines from which articles have been selected, and also to Messrs. Houghton, Mifflin, & Co., for permission to make extracts from two or three of their copyrighted works, especially from Hawthorne's Note-Books—which are not only interesting as revealing the inner workings of a rare and delicate genius, but contain a large amount of entertaining literary gossip in regard to many of his most famous contemporaries.

# CONTENTS.

| CHAPTER | | PAGE |
|---|---|---|
| I. | THOMAS CARLYLE | 1 |
| II. | GEORGE ELIOT | 41 |
| III. | JOHN RUSKIN | 58 |
| IV. | JOHN HENRY NEWMAN | 68 |
| V. | ALFRED TENNYSON | 74 |
| VI. | RALPH WALDO EMERSON | 86 |
| VII. | WILLIAM CULLEN BRYANT | 98 |
| VIII. | LONGFELLOW AND WHITTIER | 119 |
| IX. | LOWELL AND HOLMES | 135 |
| X. | NATHANIEL HAWTHORNE | 150 |
| XI. | WALT WHITMAN | 161 |
| XII. | BAYARD TAYLOR | 178 |
| XIII. | SWINBURNE AND OSCAR WILDE | 202 |
| XIV. | THE BROWNINGS | 216 |
| XV. | CHARLES DICKENS | 236 |
| XVI. | WILLIAM MAKEPEACE THACKERAY | 294 |
| XVII. | SOME YOUNGER WRITERS | 321 |

# LIST OF ILLUSTRATIONS.

|  | PAGE |
|---|---|
| THOMAS CARLYLE | *Frontispiece.* |
| JOHN RUSKIN | 58 |
| JOHN HENRY NEWMAN | 68 |
| WILLIAM CULLEN BRYANT | 98 |
| THE OLD CRAIGIE HOUSE | 122 |
| HENRY W. LONGFELLOW | 124 |
| NATHANIEL HAWTHORNE | 150 |
| BAYARD TAYLOR | 178 |
| THE TAYLOR HOMESTEAD | 188 |
| WILLIAM MAKEPEACE THACKERAY | 294 |

# CHAPTER I.

## THOMAS CARLYLE.

Manners and appearance in his early days—Margaret Fuller's portrait—Anecdotes and reminiscences—The Carlyle household described by Henry Larkin.

IN one of his "Autobiographic Sketches" De Quincey tells a story of an evening party at Coleridge's where the conversation having turned upon the Mohammedan creed, theology, and morals, some young man, introduced by Edward Irving, thought fit to pronounce a splendid eulogium upon Mahomet and all his doctrines. This, as a pleasing extravagance, had amused all present. Some hours after, when the party came to separate, the philo-Mohammedan missed his hat, upon which, while a general search for it was going on, Lamb, turning to the stranger, said, " Hat, sir? Your hat? Don't you think you came in a turban?" The story is not a particularly good one, although De Quincey quotes it with evident triumph as a notable addition to the stock of Eliana, but, as there need be no difficulty in identifying the "young man introduced by Irving," it is interesting as affording a glimpse of Carlyle in his early days. It shows, also, that in his comparatively obscure youth his sturdy self-assertion and overbearing eloquence were not to be daunted, even on a first introduction, by the most brilliant intellectual society in England. It was probably a year or two later that Carlyle was met by George Gilfillan at a party given by Jeffrey. Gilfillan describes him as a man of about thirty years of age, with dark locks approaching to a curl; cheeks tinged with a healthy red; a brow broad, prominent, but rather low, not unlike that which painters give to Burns; eyes which in a front view said nothing, but which, when seen from the side, were seen rolling in fire; lips which appeared as if perpetually champing some invisible bit; the whole aspect of the face being that of infinite restlessness, strongly restrained by self-control. His eyes and lips when he spoke seemed taking parts, and responding to each other in one wild tune. A jaw like that of a tiger formed the base of the head; and a form not tall, but commanding in its mediocrity, from an air of proud humility and half-stooping strength, finished off the whole. In a strange, wild Annandale accent he began an address: "The public," he said, "had become a gigantic jackass; Literature, a glittering lie; Science was groping aimlessly amidst the dry dead clatter of the machinery by which it means the universe; Art wielding a feeble, watery pencil; History stumbling over dry bones in a valley no longer of vision; Philosophy lisping and babbling exploded absurdities, mixed with new nonsense about the Infinite, the Absolute, and the Eternal; our Religion a great truth groaning its last; Truth, Justice, God, turned big, staring, empty words, like the address on a sign remaining after the house was abandoned, or like the envelope after the letter had been extracted, drifting down the wind. And what men we have to meet the crisis! Sir Walter Scott, a toothless retailer of old wives' fables; Brougham, an eternal grinder of commonplace and pretentious noise, like a man playing on a hurdy-gurdy; Coleridge, talking in a maudlin sleep an infinite deal of nothing; Wordsworth, stooping to extract a spiritual catsup from mushrooms which were little better than toadstools; John Wilson, taken to presiding at Noctes, and painting haggises in floods; the bishops and clergy of all denominations combined to keep men in a state of pupilage, that *they* may be kept in port wine and roast beef; politicians full of cant, insincerity, and falsehood; Peel, a plausible fox; John Wilson Croker, an unhanged hound; Lord John Russell, a turnspit of good pedigree; Lord Melbourne, a monkey; 'these be thy gods, O Israel!' Others occupied in undertakings as absurd as to seek to suck the moon out of the sky; this wind-bag yelping for liberty to the negro, and that other for the improvement of prisons; —all sham and imposture together—a giant lie —which may soon go down in hell-fire."

The best description of Carlyle, as he appeared in the fulness of his powers, is that given in the following passages from Margaret Fuller's letters to Emerson in 1846. They have often been quoted, but they are worth quoting again.

### MARGARET FULLER'S DESCRIPTION.

Of the people I saw in London, you will wish me to speak first of the Carlyles. Mr. C. came to see me at once, and appointed an evening to be passed at their house. That first time I was delighted with him. He was in a very sweet humor, full of wit and pathos, without being overbearing or oppressive. I was quite carried away with the rich flow of his discourse; the hearty, noble earnestness of his personal being brought back the charm which once was upon his writing, before I wearied of it. I admired his Scotch, his way of singing his great full sentences, so that each one was like the stanza of a narrative ballad. He let me talk now and then, enough to free my lungs and change my position, so that I did not get tired. That evening he talked of the present state of things in England, giving light, witty sketches of the men of the day, fanatics and others, and some sweet homely stories he told of things he had known of the Scotch peasantry. Of you he spoke with hearty kindness; and he told, with beautiful feeling, a story of some poor farmer or artisan in the country who on Sunday lays aside the cark and care of that dirty English world and sits reading the essays and looking upon the sea. I left him that night intending to go out very often to their house. I assure you there never was any thing so witty as Carlyle's description of ———. It was enough to kill one with laughing. I, on my side, contributed a story to his fund of anecdote on this subject, and it was fully appreciated. Carlyle is worth a thousand of you for that; he is not ashamed to laugh when he is amused, but goes on in a cordial, human fashion. The second time Mr. C. had a dinner-party, at which was a witty, French, flippant sort of man, author of a "History of Philosophy" [George Henry Lewes], and now writing a "Life of Goethe," a task for which he must be as unfit as irreligion and sparkling shallowness can make him. But he told stories admirably, and was allowed sometimes to interrupt Carlyle a little, of which one was glad, for that night he was in his more acrid mood and, though much more brilliant than on the former evening, grew wearisome to me, who disclaimed and rejected almost every thing he said. For a couple of hours he was talking about poetry, and the whole harangue was one eloquent proclamation of the defects in his own mind. Tennyson wrote in verse because the school-masters had taught him that it was great to do so, and had thus, unfortunately, been turned from the true path for a man. Burns had, in like manner, been turned from his vocation. Shakespeare had not had the good sense to see that it would have been better to write straight on in prose—and such nonsense, which, though amusing enough at first, he ran to death after a while. The most amusing part is always when he comes back to some refrain, as, in the "French Revolution," of the "sea-green." In this instance it was Petrarch and Laura, the last word pronounced with his ineffable sarcasm of drawl. Although he said this over fifty times, I could not help laughing when Laura would come,

Carlyle running his chin out when he spoke it, and his eyes glancing till they looked like the eyes and beak of a bird of prey. Poor Laura! Luckily for her that her poet had already got her safely canonized beyond the reach of this Teufelsdröckh vulture. The worst of hearing Carlyle is that you cannot interrupt him. I understand the habit and power of haranguing have increased very much upon him, so that you are a perfect prisoner when he has once got hold of you. To interrupt him is a physical impossibility. If you get a chance to remonstrate for a moment, he raises his voice and bears you down. True, he does you no injustice, and, with his admirable penetration, sees the disclaimer in your mind, so that you are not morally delinquent; but it is not pleasant to be unable to utter it. The latter part of the evening, however, he paid us for this by a series of sketches, in his finest style of railing and raillery, of modern French literature, not one of them perhaps perfectly just, but all drawn with the finest, boldest strokes, and, from his point of view, masterly. All were depreciating except that of Béranger. Of him he spoke with perfect justice, because with hearty sympathy. I had, afterward, some talk with Mrs. C., whom hitherto I had only seen, for who can speak while her husband is there? I like her very much—she is full of grace, sweetness, and talent. Her eyes are sad and charming. After this they went to stay at Lord Ashburton's, and I only saw them once more, when they came to pass an evening with us. Unluckily, Mazzini was with us, whose society, when he was there alone, I enjoyed more than any. He is a beauteous and pure music ; also, he is a dear friend of Mrs. C., but his being there gave the conversation a turn to " progress " and ideal subjects, and C. was fluent in invectives on all our " rose-water imbecilities." We all felt distant from him, and Mazzini, after some vain efforts to remonstrate, became very sad. Mrs. C. said to me, " These are but opinions to Carlyle, but to Mazzini, who has given his all, and helped bring his friends to the scaffold, in pursuit of such subjects, it is a matter of life and death." All Carlyle's talk that evening was a defence of mere force—success the test of right—if people would not behave well, put collars round their necks— find a hero, and let them be his slaves, etc. It was very Titanic and anti-celestial. I wish the last evening had been more melodious. However, I bid Carlyle farewell with feelings of the warmest friendship and admiration. We cannot feel otherwise to a great and noble nature, whether it harmonize with our own or not. I never appreciated the work he has done for his age till I saw England. I could not. . You must stand in the shadow of that mountain of shams to know how hard it is to cast light across it

*Paris, December*, 1846.—Accustomed to the infinite wit and exuberant richness of his writings, his talk is still an amazement and a splendor scarcely to be faced with steady eyes. He does not converse, only harangues. It is the usual misfortune of such marked men that they cannot allow other minds room to breathe and show themselves in their atmosphere, and thus miss the refreshment and instruction which the greatest never cease to need from the experience of the humblest. Carlyle allows no one a chance, but bears down all opposition, not only by his wit and onset of words, resistless in their sharpness as so many bayonets, but by actual physical superiority, raising his voice and rushing on his opponent with a torrent of sounds. This is not in the least from unwillingness to allow freedom to others. On the contrary, no man would more enjoy a manly resistance to his thought. But it is the nature of a mind accustomed to follow out its own impulse as the hawk its prey, and which knows not how to stop in the chase. Carlyle, indeed, is arrogant and overbearing, but in his arrogance there is no littleness, no self-love. It is the heroic arrogance of some old Scandinavian conqueror; it is his nature, and the untamable impulse that has given him power to crush the dragons. You do not love him, perhaps, nor revere; and perhaps, also, he would only laugh at you if you did; but you like him heartily, and like to see him, the powerful smith, the Siegfried, melting all the old iron in his furnace till it glows to a sunset red, and burns you if you senselessly go too near. He seems to me quite isolated, lonely as the desert; yet never was a man more fitted to prize a man, could he find one to match his mood. He finds them, but only in the past. He sings rather than talks. He pours upon you a kind of satirical, heroical, critical poem, with regular cadences, and generally catching up, near the beginning, some singular epithet, which serves as a refrain when his song is full. He sometimes stops a minute to laugh at himself, then begins anew with fresh vigor; for all the spirits he is driving before him seem to him as fata-morganas, ugly masks, in fact, if he can but make them turn about; but he laughs that they seem to others such dainty Ariels.

"Carlyle," says Mr. G. W. Smalley, of the *Tribune*, "never troubled himself about conventionalities. What he felt, that he said, and as he felt it; and it did not matter if he sat in his own room or in a public hall. At one of Dickens' readings he has been known to burst out in irrepressible, long-continued, stentorian laughter, that amounted almost to a convulsion; swinging his hat in the air meanwhile." He expressed his opinions bluntly enough.

When Mr. William Black called upon him he growled out, "Are you never going to write any thing serious?" "And now," he asked Mr. A'Beckett, the author of various "comic" histories, "when do you bring out your 'Comic Bible'?" He told a friend once that Miss Barrett (Mrs. Browning) had sent him two volumes of poems, and he had written her that "if she had any thing to say she had better put it into plain prose, so a body could understand it, and not trouble herself to make rhymes. But," he laughingly added, "the woman felt so badly about it that I had to write again." A physician asked him why he did not take medical advice for his ailments. "Sir," he shouted, "I might as well pour my troubles into the long hairy ears of a jackass as consult a member of your profession." Another story used to be told with much point by Dickens. The self-confident editor of a certain review was present at a dinner-party, and had enunciated some weighty opinion on the subject under discussion, wrapping it up in a small parcel and laying it by on a shelf as if done with forever—and a dead silence ensued. This silence, to the astonishment of all, was broken by Carlyle looking across the table at the editor in a dreamy way, and saying as though to himself, but in perfectly audible tones, "Eh, but you're a puir cratur, a puir, wratched, meeserable cratur!" Then, with a sigh, he relapsed into silence.

Of Carlyle's domestic life a very interesting glimpse has been afforded us by Mr. Henry Larkin, who was for many years an intimate friend of the household. This gentleman tells us that he had long worshipped Carlyle at a distance as the one to whom, "next to my Sovereign Lord and Master, Jesus Christ," he was most deeply indebted for light and guidance. But it was not until 1856 that he made his acquaintance. The story I give in his own words, though with some retrenchment and abridgment, to fit it within the limits of this volume.

### HENRY LARKIN'S REMINISCENCES.

I was living in London, and I chanced to learn that Carlyle wanted help. I was told that he was hard at work on Frederick the Great; and that he was also preparing to issue a collected edition of his works, for which he wanted good indexes. I saw at once that my opportunity had at length come; and that there was now a possibility of doing something really useful while I lived. I was still unmarried, and my needs were as moderate as my means, and I had my evenings as free as I chose to make them. So I wrote him a rather long letter, explaining what was necessary, and volunteering my services; upon which I received the following friendly yet cautious invitation:

*Chelsea, 14th December, 1856.*

DEAR SIR:—Your Letter is very loyal and good; your offer altogether kind and friendly. I am not without help, volunteer and hired, in these troublesome Enterprises of mine; nor is there an immediate necessity for more. But I make no doubt you, too, could do acceptable service, if you continued steadily inclined that way.

Perhaps you may as well come and see me at any rate; we shall then see better what is doable, what not. On Tuesday Evening we are at home, my Wife and I as usual; Tea is at 7½ o'clock; if I hear nothing from you, let us expect you then for an hour and half.

Believe me yours truly,

T. CARLYLE.

I smiled as I read the limitation of "an hour and half," and wondered what sort of long-winded visitor he expected to find me. Punctual to the time, I knocked at the door. I was conducted upstairs into the drawing-room; and Mrs. Carlyle, who was sitting at needlework by a small table, rose to receive me. She was very kind, but reserved, and I thought looked strangely sorrowful, as if some great trouble were weighing her down; I thought she looked ill, and yet there was evidently something more depressing than mere bodily suffering. She said Mr. Carlyle would be down presently, but had not finished his afternoon sleep; adding, in a slight tone of disparagement, "He always takes a long sleep before tea, and then complains that he can get no sleep at night." While I was wondering at this strange reception, Carlyle himself entered. He bowed somewhat ceremoniously, and we shook hands. He then bade me be seated, and tea was brought in. Of course we talked as we sipped our tea; but what I chiefly remember is the strange feeling of reserve which seemed to have taken possession of all three of us. Gradually Carlyle began to thaw, probably as he gradually perceived that he had not caught such a gushing enthusiast as he may not unreasonably have expected. At nine o'clock I made a movement, indicating that I was aware that the time allowed was up. But he again bade me be seated, kindly said there was no need to hurry away, that he always went out for a walk before bed, and that he would walk out with me. In this assurance Mrs. Carlyle kindly joined, and I again sat down, feeling considerably more at ease than before. After this the conversation became more specific, and almost genial, although I recollect very little which would be worth repeating. Mrs. Carlyle said little, merely putting in an occasional remark. At length Carlyle abruptly introduced the business which had brought me there, and which I had been waiting for him to refer to. Perhaps my face brightened at this, but certainly his own reserve there and then fell from him, and for the first time I felt that I saw Carlyle himself.

He told me the Lives of Sterling and Schiller were the first things requiring attention; and that his wish was to have a summary of each chapter and an index of both Lives, to be placed at the end of the book. That, if I found myself fit for the work, and the work fit for me, he could at least promise me enough of it. But one absolute condition was, that he himself was not to be worried about it, his thoughts being entirely absorbed in other work. In short, that superfluous talk (including writing) was, on all occasions, the one thing to be avoided. He handed me the books, and, at eleven o'clock instead of nine, we went out together. He walked with me a mile or more on my road, talking in a kind, fatherly way, which sent me home gratefully triumphant. Mrs. Carlyle was again very kind at parting; but I saw, with a feeling of perplexed disappointment, the same weary look, almost of indifference, which I had noticed when I entered. I little knew then the wearing misery of her life, and little thought how anxiously she was foreboding that all this " romantic devotion," as she afterward called it, on my part, and Carlyle's ready acceptance of it, must inevitably end in trouble to us both. This was the time which Carlyle, in his Reminiscences, so sadly speaks of, as the "nadir of her sufferings." I may as well say at once that her anxious forebodings were never quite fulfilled. Troubles enough there undoubtedly were, and, as will be seen, disappointments, too, on both sides. But I think I may confidently say that our relation was one of unbroken mutual esteem from first to last.

I set to work upon the Sterling, and, when I had finished it, sent it with a short note, thinking it best not to trouble Carlyle by calling until he had looked at it and wished to see me, especially as I still had the Schiller to go on with it. While preparing the index, etc., I noted two or three little points which seemed dubious, and called attention to them by slips of paper between the leaves, on which I wrote only what was necessary, thinking it would thus be very little trouble for him to glance at the page, and then do any thing or nothing as he saw fit. There was nothing of any great importance. He had spoken of Sterling in his first few years as being still in "long clothes;" and I pointed out that this was a form of expression usually applied by mothers to the bird-of-paradise apparel in which they adorn their infants before there is any possibility of the little feet alighting on the ground, and was hardly applicable to a boy trotting by his father's side. I also called attention to an extract which had evidently been tucked in after the rest was written, and which wanted some slight grammatical dovetailing. Besides this, there were two or three instances of what seemed to be imperfect punctuation.

I went next week as desired ; and was much delighted at the cordiality with which both Carlyle and Mrs. Carlyle received me. I was especially surprised and delighted at the change in Mrs. Carlyle. She had been very kind before, but with a patiently hopeless look, like a mourner standing by an unclosed grave. But all this had now passed away. All the blinds were drawn up in her house of mourning; and her face was illuminated with the brightest of welcomes. I never knew any one who could deal out little flatteries so pleasantly and judiciously. I have seen it administered by the spoonful, like brimstone and treacle, and even laid on copiously, as if with a plasterer's trowel. But she knew better. She knew the sensitive points exactly, and, if she chose, could touch them so delicately that it almost seemed like a happy inadvertence ; and she could also prick them with the deftest of needles, if she saw fit. She expressed a good deal of bantering astonishment at what she called "my accurate knowledge of baby-linen," and was altogether cheerful and congratulatory.

After this my visits became less formal, and were entirely pleasant and encouraging. Mrs. Carlyle and I seemed to get on very happily together. She said she didn't see why Carlyle (she always called him "Carlyle" when in her best moods) should have me all to himself; and enlisted my services in many little practical difficulties of her own. She once, in those early days, told me, in her pleasant half-flattering, half-bantering way, that I was "the only one she had ever heard Carlyle speak of without what Sir Robert Peel would call 'mitigating circumstances'!" After some little time, I ventured to send him a short essay of mine, "The Poetry of Life," which had appeared in *Chambers's Journal* previous to my Carlylean era, in which I had endeavored to express my notion of the Christian ideal. It was not that I attached any special value to the essay; but I thought, flimsy as it might seem to him, it would at least show him my own ethical stand-point, and might call forth some observations from him which would be of value to me, and might even lead to a closer communion of thought between us. The next time I went, after we had transacted our business and I was about to leave (for it was only a passing call, in the early part of the day), he returned me my little paper, with a serious, almost grieved look, but without a word of comment. Mrs. Carlyle was equally silent; and I had to go my way, pondering what such omens might portend. I see now clearly enough that, even in those early days, they must already have looked on me as a kind of feeble Irving; with much of his spirit of willing helpfulness, but utterly without his great gifts, for which perhaps chiefly they had both admired him. I have no doubt they were sincerely grieved at the thought, that here was another earnest life brought close to them, equally bound to be wrecked in the vain struggle after the impossible and unattainable. In our subsequent intercourse Mrs. Carlyle tried, many times and in many ways, to impress on me a wholesome sense of all such disastrous futilities. Carlyle seemed as yet to content himself with absolute silence on such impracticable topics; probably waiting for some freer opportunity, and perhaps hoping that a course of steady hard work might of itself grind much of it out of me. But I shall have to recur to this subject hereafter. Of course all this was not conducive to any very free sympathy of thought or feeling. Indeed, I soon found, even in our freest moments, that there was a distinct distance between us which neither could genially cross.

While on the subject of indexes and summaries, I may perhaps be pardoned for saying that they cost me far more labor than Carlyle had any idea of. But I got my own advantage out of the work, and never left any passage until I was satisfied that I had got the full meaning of it.

At the time of which I am now writing, while I

was thus struggling with work which I wholly liked and appreciated, the ill-luck of weary and utterly incompatible labor, which has dogged my footsteps through life, was already barking at the door. One day I found Carlyle in great tribulation of spirit about maps and battle-plans, which had become necessary to illustrate the *Frederick*, then seething and sputtering on the anvil at the fiercest white heat; and which maps and plans he had found himself quite unable to arrange. He had tried his hand at them, and had at last thrown them from him in utter loathing and despair; and now wistfully appealed to me, to say "whether amongst my many facilities of help, even map-making might not possibly be one." I never listened to any appeal with feelings of more real dismay than I listened then. I knew well that, do what I would, the whole thing would be as unconquerably intolerable to me as it had already proved to himself. I had had long and very bitter experience, not of map-making and battle-plans, but of very kindred employment; and I knew with inward shuddering what it must mean for me. But what was I to do? Was I to refuse him, and throw him back upon his own despair, when he was so confidently and really so pathetically looking to me for deliverance? "No," I thought; "I have put my hand to the work; and I will push through with it, come what may!"

I never saw Carlyle look so really grateful as when,

with many misgivings, I promised to try what I could do. But from that time my labors with him were almost as weary a struggle as his own. My only satisfaction in now looking back upon them is that, notwithstanding all my repugnances, I did succeed; and gave him almost perfect satisfaction in every instance. So irksome to me was the misery they inflicted, that in after-years I could never hear him refer to them (as he often gratefully did, as the one thing in which I had really helped him) without a twinge of pain; partly, I confess, of disappointment that it should be what I cared for least that he valued and remembered best.

During all this time, as may be supposed, I was a frequent visitor at Cheyne Row; and afterward, much more so. I generally looked in in the forenoon, that time being usually most convenient to me. My practice was to go straight up to Carlyle in his sky-lighted study, and arrange whatever matter I had to consult him about; and then, as I passed down, have half an hour's chat with Mrs. Carlyle in the drawing-room. They were generally very pleasant half-hours.

It must have been about this time, too, that I gradually became alive to the intense dreariness of her own life. She had such a perfect mastery of herself, and such a stoical resolution to shut in her own misery from the eyes of the world, that I suppose not many even of her intimate friends ever

knew how much she was actually suffering. It was
not merely the feeling of utter loneliness, arising
from Carlyle's moody absorption in his own work.
All this, I believe, she could have borne without
flinching. Indeed, she had such an unshaken faith
in his genius, and such a queenly appreciation of
her own prerogatives as his wife, that I am convinced she would not, even at the worst, have exchanged her lowly position for the highest in the
land. I cannot for a moment suppose that their
two lives were really blended into one. How, on
such terms, could they be? But she was by no
means deficient in that last infirmity of female
hearts, a jealous sense of "property" in her husband, of which all poachers would do well to be-
ware. She showed also a true feminine intolerance
for any thing in her own sex which she did not herself understand; especially if it aimed at an ideal
with which she had no sympathy: as was indeed
almost unpardonably her case with regard to Irving's true-hearted and devoted wife; as Carlyle
himself, unconsciously, yet too plainly, and even
cruelly, testifies. Yet, I venture to believe, she
would have been as much shocked as any one at his
incredibly bitter fanatical "anti-fanatic" version of
it. "Oh, those 'unspeakable' men," I can fancy
her exclaiming, almost with horror, "how stupidly
blundering they are, taking every silly thing so
dreadfully in earnest!" There had, too, been some

superficial love-passages between Irving and herself in their young days; and I can quite believe this also may have given piquancy to her feeling of antagonism. No one who knew her can doubt that she would fully appreciate the triumph of having once had the choice between two such men; and, with all her almost invincible heroism, she evidently had not quite magnanimity enough to generously forget it. I always think that any woman who can amuse herself and friends by talking of such tempting little victories could not have been altogether incapable of some little tantalizing complicity in bringing them about! At the time I knew her, she possessed plenty of resources of her own, and friends and acquaintances in more than abundance; and she well knew how to hold her own in all wordy warfare, and give tit for tat all round with sparkling vivacity. She had also a mischievous delight in treading on the delicate toes of the conventional proprieties; and I have heard her say the most audacious things with a look of demure unconsciousness, which would have broken out into the pleasantest, or sharpest, mocking astonishment, if you were simple enough to profess being shocked. She sometimes tried those shafts at me, to see whether I would wince; especially with reference to what she was pleased to call my "youthful enthusiasms," and even more serious matters. But when I saw her deftly aim them, I generally allowed them to glance past me, being no match for her with that kind of swift, sharp-pointed artillery. Once she told me "it was mostly mad people who came running after Carlyle," leaving me to make my own application. It must have been on one of these occasions that she mentioned, as a kind of general remark, " what a comfort it was sometimes to have stupid people about you, it saved so much trouble !" All this sort of thing, I should say, she fully enjoyed, while it was alive and on the wing; but, when she was again solitary, the reaction was proportionate. It was not, as I said, merely Carlyle's absorption in his work which weighed on her spirit; she knew this was inevitable, and would have cheerfully faced it, if only for the vantage-ground it gave her with the world. The misery was to be shut up alone with him, when he himself was struggling under his burdens in utter wretchedness and gloominess of heart. When his dark labor-pains were strong upon him, I suppose he was the most absolutely wretched man I ever saw. Even to stand firmly on one's own feet in the presence of such misery and consequent irritability, was well-nigh impossible. But what she felt most keenly of all was, that he never seemed to realize that misery is the most contagious of all diseases. He saw her always invincibly devoted to him ; and he thought her lot peaceful and happy in comparison with his own. He never saw the misery his own misery was inflicting upon her and gradually sapping the very life out of her. I have heard her, many times, speak of their life at Craigenputtoch with absolute shuddering; and I do not wonder when they left at her gayly proposing to "burn our ships" and so prevent the possibility of return! I once took an opportunity of referring to what Sterling had said about her skill in writing, and ventured to wonder that she did not still try to find a little amusement in that way. But she shut me up very sharply by saying, "Oh, Mr. Larkin, one writer is quite enough in a house." And yet, I ought to say, I never once heard an angry word pass between themselves. If Carlyle had not himself written so frankly of these things, I should never have dared to write what I am now writing. I have hardly spoken of them to any one, for I felt them to be troubles which God only could be trusted with; but they sank very deeply and sorrowfully into my own heart. She was anxious, too, about me, and often warned me that I was looking for a recognition which I should never gain. By this time, notwithstanding Carlyle's very kind and hearty appreciation of my poor services, I had begun to see rather deeply into the inevitable truth of this gentlest friendly foreboding. Even Carlyle's praise, always frankly conscientious, was far too serious and admonitory ever to be lightly accepted like Mrs. Carlyle's playful flatteries. They always seemed to tacitly imply, "This is my clear and emphatic approval, so far. Take heed that you continue to deserve it." In fact, I not unfrequently recalled his own grim words: "Hardly for the flower of men will love alone do; and for the scoundrelism of men it has not even a chance to do." He evidently thought it was something to stand clear of that latter category.

I never knew a man more free from all personal vulgarities of any kind, or one whose presence carried with it such clear unassuming dignity of manhood; which I can only describe as a certain royal graciousness of manner, as different from a spirit of condescension as wisdom is different from personal pretentiousness. He had, too, on all occasions, such a graphic discernment of all the facts he knew, and such a world-wide wealth of knowledge to liberally dispense, that few "kingdoms" have been more grandly real or more honestly won. His very failings were of a kingly order, and almost compelled respect by their absolute and evident sincerity. Of his mocking Berserker hilarity, and overwhelming power of speech when roused by worthy opposition, we have often been told; but, for my own part, I greatly preferred his half-silences, when one seemed to commune with his heart rather than with his head. At such times of quiet converse I have sometimes known him as simple, as gentle, and as open to conviction as any child. It is the recollection of such moments that keeps his memory so reverently dear to many friends, often constrained to differ from him, and even to put a higher interpretation than his own on the very truths he had taught them. Both Carlyle and Mrs. Carlyle had singularly expressive voices, and yet singularly different from each other, like the many tones of a powerful organ and the perfect modulations of a mellow flute. They both spoke heartily, with their genuine native accents, but with the easy grace of cultivated sincerity, and with no other rusticity of manner than daring to be true to the soil from which they sprang. They simply brought with them, into the midst of the French-polished upholstery of London conventional life, a vocal memory of the fresh breezes and living echoes of their own mountain streams, pine-trees, and thousand-tinted heather. But I should say that, even in his most genial moods, there was never any thing we could call really "playful" in Carlyle's thoughts or way of looking at things, as there so often was in his wife's. I can hardly imagine that even in childhood he ever practically knew the meaning of happy "play" —the pretty innocent skipping of kids and lambs, the simple bubbling-over of the cup of joy! I can only picture him as "weary and heavy laden" from his birth. Laughter he had of many kinds ; scornful, genial, triumphant ; and even a strangely sympathetic laugh of reproving pity ; but I should say, never the clear ring of overflowing heartfelt joy. Even his humor, richly abundant as it was, was never playful, like Shakespeare's, or like Thackeray's at his best ; but always either grim, or sadly pitiful, or else merely grotesquely admonitory. No sunny glances of childlike mirth and innocence ever sported within the sanctuary of his grimly earnest soul ; more like a warning iridescence playing around purgatorial fires, half revealing and half concealing the incommunicable reality, was the grimly pathetic banter in which he so frequently shrouded the message his soul felt bound to deliver. "My friends, I do not laugh," he says once ; "truly I am more inclined to weep.".

With all this grim earnestness I do not suppose Mrs. Carlyle ever had any deep or real sympathy ; and I sometimes think she may once have greatly over-estimated her own ability to rally him out of it. Perhaps she never altogether gave up the attempt. She was always very ready with playful surprises whenever a fair occasion served. One morning, after I had finished my business upstairs, I looked in at the drawing-room as usual, when she asked me whether Carlyle had mentioned "that little paper he was to speak to me about." I said, "No ; but that I supposed he had forgotten it and that I would go back to inquire." I went back : but Carlyle knew no more about it than I did. At last he got up from his table, where he was busily writing, and came down to ask her what it was. I followed him. She let us get close up to her table where she also was writing; and then held up before us a slip of paper upon which, while I was gone, she had written—"The 1st of April!" Carlyle and I looked at each other, laughing heartily at our mutual bewilderment; and he then strode off, and returned upstairs to his study. Whereupon she was highly triumphant at having, as she said, "brought down *two* such philosophers with one shot!"

Once I recollect a bantering allusion to "Carlyle's friends, the immortal gods!" but I forget what the occasion was. She never hesitated about quizzing him, just as she did every one else; and I noticed that he always seemed to rather like it. Once he was giving me some little bit of copying or map-making to do, and was elaborately impressing on me the importance of dispatch, but at the same time, of there being no actual hurry about it; which was a way he had, like touching up with the whip and holding in with the bridle at the same moment. I intimated my perfect understanding of his wishes; and quoted Goethe's well-known words, which had once made a deep impression on me, "like a star, unhasting and unresting." "Ah," interposed Mrs. Carlyle, "Carlyle is always hasting, and *never* resting;" which, indeed, was the saddest fact of both their lives. She was once very severe upon what she called Goethe's "hard heart." "No one," she said, "but a hard-hearted man, could have treated a pathetic character like poor little Mignon as *he* had treated her. If, for the sake of his story, he was bound to kill her, at least he was not bound to make stuffy speeches about it, and—embalm her!" Meanwhile Carlyle looked on benignly, as if he were listening to some pretty innocent prattle, but said nothing. I recollect the interest excited at the publication of "Adam Bede," and how much Mrs. Carlyle was amused with the character of Mrs. Poyser. She told me Carlyle had read two or three chapters, and then threw the book down; refusing, for some reason of his own, to look at it again.

I find my presentation copy of the first two volumes of "Frederick" inscribed "with many thanks and regards, 30th September, 1858." When he handed me the volumes, Carlyle solemnly and impressively thanked me for the great and unexpected help I had given him in his heavy labor, without which he shuddered to think where he might then have been. I cannot recall all that he said; but the words—" with a luminous silence, and a steady fidelity of effort, beyond all his experience or imagination; if it would be any satisfaction to me to know it,"—have remained with me as if spoken but yesterday. He then kindly insisted on my acceptance of a check (£100), and accompanied it with many earnest wishes for my future welfare.

In addition to map-making, my labors had gradually come to include the deciphering and copying-out of the more intricate and least intelligible bits of Carlyle's sometimes singularly intricate manuscript. I recollect, on one occasion, he had been worrying himself, almost beyond endurance, over some unusually refractory specimen which had stubbornly resisted every attempt to force it into shape, when to his relief I entered his study. He at once handed me the page of hieroglyphics to take away and make a fair copy of; saying, with a kind of self-mocking, self-pitying laugh, "*I* cannot make out the sense of it, but I have no doubt *you* will be able!" On another occasion, on handing me a similar piece, he said despairingly, it was " almost like asking for the interpretation, without even giving me the dream!" I was always thoroughly interested in this kind of work, which had for me nothing of the intense dreariness of battle-plans and map-making. It was especially interesting to me to find how I could sometimes, as it were, meet his thought half-way, and see what he was trying to express, even before I had got all the words together. But I was not very ready at it either; I seldom could do this sort of thing at a glance. I generally had to puzzle and brood over it, until the idea seemed almost to come of its own accord. As I said, Carlyle never realized how much trouble these things sometimes cost me, nor did I care to speak much of it. In fact, as a rule, it was of no use talking to him about trouble; it only made him disinclined to trouble you.

By this time I had removed to Brompton, chiefly for the purpose of being nearer to Cheyne Row. Of course I was now frequently there, generally looking in some three or four times a week. Occasionally I spent the evening there, in which case I always joined Carlyle in his eleven-o'clock walk. Those quiet walks I felt to be a great privilege, and generally found them highly profitable; but sometimes not so profitable. I had all along been tacitly and uncomfortably conscious that both he and Mrs. Carlyle were greatly concerned about me, lest I should persist in wasting my life in mere spiritual abnegations. On one occasion, I suppose, he felt constrained to clear his own conscience toward me, as he has since told us he once did toward Irving. I well recollect his speaking to me of Irving in very sorrowful and affectionate terms; of his great gifts; his truthful, affectionate, and courageous heart; and how it was all wasted and wrecked on the maddest of futilities, ending only in a heart-broken half-consciousness that his life had been a disastrous mistake. He also told me that he had been credibly informed that, toward the end of it all, he had been heard to lament how different it might all have been if he had kept nearer to himself; or at least (as he conscientiously explained) that was the conclusion he had himself drawn from what he had been told. It was in no spirit of boasting, or of proud self-sufficiency, that this was spoken; but in the deepest sorrow and pity; and, at the time, I had no doubt whatever of its being the simple fact, although I am now convinced that it was almost an entire misunderstanding on his part. Self-reproach Irving may have felt in his own sensitive conscience, that he had not been more faithful in his testimony to his early friend; but assuredly few "last days" were more tragically *un*faltering than his. I knew, from the time Carlyle began to speak, "for quickly comes such knowledge," that he was trying to teach me by a parable; and I would gladly have set his mind at rest about me. But I could not feel that his impressive parable had any real bearing on my case. I felt we were both reaching out to each other in the dark; ineffectually, and to our mutual disapointment.

On another occasion he referred in terms of utter condemnation to the subject of so-called "spiritualism"; evidently wishful to know how I regarded it. I said the basest thing about it was its miserable attempt to turn the awful *stillness* of Eternity into a penny peep-show. He entirely agreed with me; and yet I could see that my rejoinder was not what he wanted. He wanted me to declare my total disbelief in the whole thing. But this, with the Bible before me, I was not prepared to do. We had many little tentative encounters of this kind, but never got to any actual disputation. Once he spoke in strong disparagement of the pitiful inconsistency of some one, I forget now who it was, professing to believe in his teaching, and *also* in the nonsense taught in the name of religion. But this again was far too widely aimed to touch me, and I let it pass. Why should I feel called upon to defend generally the "nonsense" of so-called religion, when my life had been a struggle to gain, if possible, its practical and living wisdom? I never could talk with him freely and unreservedly on such subjects. I always had an uncomfortable perception that there was a whole world of thought, to me of more than vital moment, which to him was as nothing. How then could we wisely talk about it? I also felt that he himself had a kind of wounded consciousness of something of the kind; and that he sometimes even resented it as "the unkindest cut of all." Of course all this arose as much from my own faultiness as from his. I often longed earnestly enough to talk frankly with him; but my own ideas were still far from being clearly defined. Many thoughts and purposes were rising and jostling against each other in my mind, which refused to take shape; and Carlyle was not a man to go to with a bewildered and bewildering difficulty, especially a difficulty beyond his own power to solve. This was precisely my case; and it was the one sore point between us at which we continually touched. I see now that he must have felt more deeply hurt at this palpable want of faith in him, than at the time, in my seeming insignificance, I could at all have imagined. "Here, at last," he must at such times have thought, "a disciple has come to me who evidently understands my God-given message; and yet even he has only a half-hearted belief in me!" The fact is, it was enough for me then, as in so many other cases of perplexity and doubt, to fall back on his own wise words: "'Do, with all thy might, what thy hand findeth to do'; speak of the same only to the infinitesimal few,—nay, oftenest to nobody, not even to thyself!" These words, when I first read them, sank very deep into my heart. And yet, I must confess, I also, for my own part, could not help feeling somewhat hurt and disappointed. "Here was I, striving to live faithfully in my own poor way according to his own wise teaching; and, because I was not, what he had so strenuously warned me against, a glib talker or mere intellectual coruscation of any kind, but had my own silent distresses and perplexities to struggle with, he was dissatisfied with me!"

Generally speaking, this sore feeling was altogether tacit and unacknowledged between us; and I even doubt whether he knew that I was distinctly conscious of it. It was not a thing we could well have spoken of: we could only have hoped to mutually outlive it. But on two occasions, and only two, perhaps while suffering from more than ordinary constitutional irritability, he quite lost all wise control of himself, and showed me, in a momentary flash of anger, what I would gladly never have looked upon, but which was far too significant to be honestly omitted. One morning, when I entered his study, I found him as usual sitting at his table, but evidently in a condition of great suppressed irritability, with Mill's treatise "On Liberty" lying before him ; which some one, perhaps Mill himself, had sent him. I believe the book had recently been published, but I cannot say positively. Certainly I had until then never seen it, or heard of it. After I had discharged my trifling business, he rose angrily from the table with the book in his hand, and gave vent to such a torrent of anathema (glancing at Christianity itself, as if Christianity had been the inspiration of it) as filled me with pain and amazement. He addressed himself directly to me, almost as if *I* had written the book, or had sent it to him, or was in some way mixed up with it in his mind. I felt terribly hurt, but what could I say in protest against such a wide-rushing torrent of invective ? I had never read the book, and did not know how far I might agree with it, or even whether I might not execrate it in my own heart as utterly as he did. Neither did he expressly charge me with any complicity with its ideas. But he did, in his haste, say things which he ought not to have said, and which, I am sure, we both, afterward, painfully wished had never been spoken. In fact, I could see that he was even tragically sorry, almost as soon as his constitutional irritability had thus found unlicensed vent. I do not think that I made him any direct response. We parted soon after in perfect friendliness; but, too palpably, another shadow had fallen between us.

The second occasion to which I have referred occurred long afterward, and was altogether trivial in comparison; a mere straw marking the hidden disturbance of the stream upon which it floated. This time it was in the drawing-room, and Mrs. Carlyle was present. He was asking me to do some trifling mechanical service for him, similar to what I had done once before, and, lest I should have forgotten, proceeded to give me altogether wrong instructions. Of course I corrected his mistake, and explained to him how the thing had really been done; but I could see that he was not altogether himself, and I know I spoke as tenderly as I could. Perhaps even this touched him painfully and gave offence; as if I were assuming to have more self-control than he had. Anyhow, he only grew more and more irritable, as I tried to convince him that it could not possibly be done in the way he said. He stormily insisted that he was right, and that *he surely* ought to know. We were both standing looking at each other, I sorrowfully knowing that mechanism would not alter its conditions to please either of us; and he, in his loose-fitting coat, and with his long sceptre-like pipe admonitorily sweeping the air, angrily and utterly refusing to be convinced. He finished by saying, in strangely measured, sarcastic cadences, "It may — be perfectly—credible—to *you*—that I am entirely—devoid of sense," and then impatiently left the room. Mrs. Carlyle and I looked at each other in despair. Meanwhile he had betaken himself to the garden, to try to smoke off his irritation. I think I have seldom been more reverently affected, and even humbled, than when, in about five or ten minutes, he again entered the room, frankly admitting his error, and expressing his great regret that he should have allowed himself to be so carried away. I have often thought of this sterling honesty and touching self-correction in so great a man, and have lately remembered it in his behalf, while reading the similarly hasty outpourings of his feverishly troubled heart, which have been so unreservedly published and so angrily criticised—

> No reckoning made, but set to his account
> With all their imperfections on his head.

In 1862 I married and, mainly at Mrs. Carlyle's instigation, took the house, No. 6, next door to him, which was then falling vacant. We all thought this would prove a very convenient and pleasant arrangement; but I soon found that it was a mistake, so far as I was concerned. Carlyle had become so accustomed to apply to me in every little difficulty, that, now that it could be done so conveniently, it grew to be a very serious tax upon my time, without giving me the satisfaction of feeling that it was at all of corresponding advantage to him. Mrs. Carlyle continued as sorrowfully and as kindly affectionate as ever: but I felt more and more distinctly that I should never get nearer to himself by more frequent intercourse. On the contrary, his spirit of irritability and impatience became more frequent, and I have no doubt more unconscious on his part, the more outwardly familiar we became; and I often had painful misgivings as to how far I was justified in thus giving way to him. But there was really no help for it, except by weakly leaving him in the lurch and deserting him in the midst of his difficulties. But the thought of Mrs. Carlyle's deplorable position in such a case would of itself have been enough to have prevented such a thing, even if my own spirit had broken down. From first to last my position with Carlyle was that of a friendly volunteer, anxious to render him all the help in my power; and I much doubt whether so long and so intimate a connection would have been possible on any other terms. But it must not be supposed that he allowed me to render all these services altogether for nothing. I have already mentioned the first check, and the very friendly way in which he insisted on my accepting it. After this there were several presents of £50, handed or posted to me, as occasion served, in a spirit of no less friendliness.

After the completion of the general index—having faithfully struggled with him, almost with my life in my hands, through what Mrs. Carlyle well called "the Valley of the Shadow of Frederick"—I considered my long apprenticeship to Carlyle fairly and honorably ended. There were many little friendly services which I still continued to render. Perhaps for some time I was there almost as frequently as before; and certainly we never afterward met in any other spirit than that of the friendliest cordiality  But in 1866 Mrs. Carlyle died; and Carlyle's life seemed to have suddenly become altogether downcast, haggard, and motiveless. I little knew then the helpless, hopeless, "late remorse of love," which was almost breaking his heart; and still less could I have realized that he and his really loved wife had been living side by side for so many years, and he as unconscious as the inaccessible rocks of the misery that very unconsciousness was daily and hourly inflicting.

## CHAPTER II.

### GEORGE ELIOT (Mrs. Mary Anne Evans Lewes).

Kate Field's sketch—Her timidity and reserve—Testimony of a personal friend—Various reminiscences.

IT was Miss Kate Field, we believe, who gave to the world the first "Pen-picture" of that wonderful woman who called herself "George Eliot." Writing from Florence in 1864, she told the readers of the *Atlantic Monthly* that she had just met Mrs. Lewes at the Villino Trollope, and described her as follows.

#### A NEWSPAPER SKETCH.

In heaviness of jaw and height of cheek-bone she greatly resembles a German, nor are her features unlike those of Wordsworth, judging from his pictures. The expression of her face is gentle and amiable, while her manner is particularly timid and retiring. In conversation Mrs. Lewes is most entertaining, and her interest in young writers is a trait which immediately takes captive all persons of this class. We shall not forget with what kindness and earnestness she addressed a young girl who had just begun to handle a pen, how frankly she related her own literary experience, and how gently she suggested advice. True genius is always allied to humanity, and in seeing Mrs. Lewes do the work of a good Samaritan so unobtrusively, we learned to respect the woman as much as we had ever admired the writer. "For years," said she to us, "I wrote reviews because I knew too little of humanity."

George Eliot in her lifetime maintained a self-respecting privacy. She never allowed herself to be "interviewed"; she shrank from having her personality made a subject of discussion in the press. No doubt she would gladly, if she could, have preserved her incognito intact and have shielded her real self behind her pen-name. Even to her friends she rarely spoke of herself. "I visited at Lewes'," says a correspondent of the *Literary World*, "and so had an acquaintance with that gifted lady for whom I felt (and feel) a sorrowful sympathy more than for any other woman. I conjecture much about her, but we shall *never* know the truth as to her early life. It was one of acute suffering from being oppressed and misunderstood, and I am certain only of this—the fact that she was more sinned against than sinning. She was indeed a reserved and silent woman. I have been with her and Lewes alone; and I know how she conversed in the privacy of her own fireside. Little, indeed, did she ever say, and what she did say was (as they phrase it in Scotland) *in print:* every word clean cut and perfectly enunciated. She asked questions (like Miss Dartle) and carefully received the answers. I have seen her, too, in company with ladies of position and rank, and heard her speak both English and French. She did not, however, shut herself up. She *received*, and was well known to (not *by*), every man of position in science, philosophy, poetry, art, and literature."

Her wishes have been respected even since her death. No flood-tide of reminiscences, such as usually follow the decease of a noted character, have been let loose upon the world by her friends. The few articles of a personal character which have made their appearance have been entirely free from gossip; they have touched only upon those traits and incidents which were not too sacredly individual to be commented upon in public. From the articles of this nature I shall present a couple of selections, but I make way first for the following chatty letter, which represents about all the particulars that even a clever and inquisitive Yankee journalist could gather in her lifetime regarding her person and habits.

George Eliot [wrote a correspondent of the *Chicago Times* in 1868] is a woman who must have passed her tenth lustrum. Despite this, her hair, a light brown, has none of those silver threads which one might expect where the burden of over half a century of years is superimposed by incessant labor and by experience full of desolation. She is not handsome. Her face is long, pale, with a small sensitive mouth. Her eyes are a vivid, warm blue-gray, full of depth, now keenly perceptive, now dreamily introspective, always full of sadness. Her hair, worn low, gives a womanly effect to a finely intellectual forehead. Her general expression is that of wearied sensitiveness whose development touches so closely on suffering that they merge into each other, leaving it doubtful where the one ends or the other begins. Despite its sadness and suggestions of suffering, it is a face full of resolute determination. This quality, however, seems the dominancy of pure will-power. Her slender figure has no expression of robust energy. Her will seems far in excess of her physical capacities;

and her energy is thus an intellectual instead of a physical fact. She is, in spite of her sensitive suggestions, full of a grand repose. Her voice is low and penetrating; and she is scarcely without exception one of the greatest of living conversationalists. "Do you know George Eliot well?" I inquired of a well-known essayist. "Yes, I do." "What is your estimate of her?" "Well, I'll tell you. I am in a position where I often meet such people as Huxley, Tyndall, Browning, and others. I am not afraid to meet them, for I may say without any vanity that I am their peer. But with George Eliot it is different. She knows more than I do. I *am* afraid of *her*. She knows every thing. History, philosophy, ancient and modern, all sciences and languages, are known to her. She is the most accomplished amateur pianiste in England." "And so you think—" "I think she is the most adorable woman that ever lived." What the witty Mrs. Trench once said of Madame de Staël, that "she is consolingly ugly," will apply to George Eliot, with the reservation, however, that her plain features are so sanctified by her expression that she becomes a very beautiful woman. She is morbidly sensitive in regard to her appearance and certain phases of her life. She has been offered fabulous sums by London photographers if she would sit for her picture, but she has always refused. She goes little or not at all into society, but has weekly receptions to which only a certain class is admitted. She may be often seen at the classical matinées given every Saturday at St. James' Hall ; and occasionally she may be seen in the street with a pair of spanking bays, a very swell carriage, and liveried servants. Her home life is a charming one. She exercises an active supervision and develops a most comprehensive management and exquisite taste in every detail of the household. In composition she is very slow and methodical, writing, I have been assured, not more than from forty to sixty lines a day. When a book is completed she is in such a state of nervous exhaustion that her husband takes her to Italy or southern France to recuperate. While writing, she must be scrupulously arranged as to person, while every detail of her surroundings must be in harmonious taste.

### PEN PICTURE BY C. KEGAN PAUL.

Mr. C. Kegan Paul, who enjoyed the privilege of a personal acquaintance with this gifted woman, has given, in a recent number of *Harper's Monthly*, the most vivid of all the descriptions of her personal appearance in the following paragraphs.

Perhaps no one filling a large portion of the thoughts of the public in two hemispheres has ever been so little known to the public at large. Always in delicate health, always living a student life, caring little for what is called general society, though taking a genial delight in that of her chosen friends, she very seldom appeared in public. She went to the houses of but a few, finding it less fatiguing to see her friends at home. Those who knew her by sight beyond her own immediate circle did so from seeing her take her quiet drives in Regent's Park and the northern slopes of London, or from her attendance at those concerts at which the best music of the day was to be heard. There, in a front row, in rapt attention, were always to be seen Mr. and Mrs. Lewes, and none who saw that face ever forgot its power and spiritual beauty. To the casual observer there was but little of what is generally understood to be beauty of form.

In more than one striking passage in his novels, Mr. Hardy has recognized the fact that the beauty of the future, as the race is more developed in intellect, can not be the ideal physical beauty of the past; and in one of the most remarkable he says that "ideal physical beauty is incompatible with mental development and a full recognition of the coil of things. Mental luminousness must be fed with the oil of life, even though there is already a physical need for it." And this was the case with George Eliot. The face was one of a group of four, not all equally like each other, but all of the same spiritual family, and with a curious interdependence of likeness. These four are Dante, Savonarola, Cardinal Newman, and herself. We only know one such other group, and that consisting of three only. It is that formed of the traditional head of Christ (the well-known profile on a coin), Shakespeare, and St. Ignatius Loyola. In the group of which George Eliot was one there is the same straight wall of brow; the droop of the powerful nose; mobile lips, touched with strong passion kept resolutely under control; a square jaw, which would make the face stern were it not counteracted by the sweet smile of lips and eye. We can hardly hope that posterity will ever know her from likenesses as those who had the honor of her acquaintance knew her in life. Only some world's artist could have handed her down as she lived, as Bellini has handed down the Doge whom we all know so well on the walls of the National Gallery. The two or three portraits that exist, though valuable, give but a very imperfect presentment. The mere shape of the head would be the despair of any painter. It was so grand and massive that it would scarcely be possible to represent it without giving the idea of disproportion to the frame, of which no one ever thought for a moment when they saw her, although it was a surprise, when she stood up, to see that, after all, she was but a little fragile woman who bore this weight of brow and brain.

It is difficult for any one admitted to the great honor of friendship with either Mr. Lewes or

George Eliot to speak of their home without seeming intrusive, in the same way that he would have been who, unauthorized, introduced visitors, yet something may be said to gratify a curiosity which surely is not now impertinent or ignoble. When London was full, the little drawing-room in St. John's Wood was now and then crowded to overflowing with those who were glad to give their best of conversation, of information, and sometimes of music, always to listen with eager attention to whatever their hostess might say, when all that she said was worth hearing. Without a trace of pedantry, she led the conversation to some great and lofty strain. Of herself and her works she never spoke; of the works and thoughts of others she spoke with reverence, and sometimes even too great tolerance. But those afternoons had the highest pleasure when London was empty or the day wet, and only a few friends were present, so that her conversation assumed a more sustained tone than was possible when the rooms were full of shifting groups. It was then that, without any premeditation, her sentences fell as fully formed, as wise, as weighty, as epigrammatic, as any to be found in her books. Always ready, but never rapid, her talk was not only good in itself, but it encouraged the same in others, since she was an excellent listener, and eager to hear. Yet interesting as seemed to her, as well as to those admitted to them, her afternoons in London, she was always glad to escape when summer came, either for one of the tours on the Continent in which she so delighted, or lately to the charming home she had made in Surrey. She never tired of the lovely scenery about Witley, and the great expanse of view obtainable from the tops of the many hills. It was on one of her drives in that neighborhood that a characteristic conversation took place between her and one of the greatest English poets, whom she met as he was taking a walk. Even that short interval enabled them to get into somewhat deep conversation on evolution; and as the poet afterward related it to a companion on the same spot, he said: "Here was where I said 'good-by' to George Eliot; and as she went down the hill, I said, 'Well, good-by, you and your molecules,' and she said to me, 'I am quite content with my molecules.'" A trifling anecdote, perhaps, but to those who will read between the lines, not other than characteristic of both speakers.

### PERSONAL REMINISCENCES BY ONE WHO KNEW HER.

George Eliot was too great a woman to be guilty of any menial Phariseeism. She was entirely free from that small scorn for the ordinary run of humanity which some of the weaker brethren of the pen think proper to assume. In her own household she laid upon herself the lowliest duties, not only with cheerfulness, but with a reverent sense of their importance. She prided herself upon being an excellent housekeeper, she was a loyal friend, a tender and affectionate parent to her husband's children. The author of a remarkable article in the *Contemporary Review*, which was simply signed as "By one who knew her," dwells at some length upon this feature of her character.

There was no taint of intellectual aristocracy [says this writer] in her sympathies. She once said, in referring to Mendelssohn's visit to England, that the musician's power to move the crowd with a visible thrill of enthusiasm would have been the object of her aspiration, had she been allowed her choice of the form her genius might have taken. The yearning seemed an expression of that respectfulness for ordinary mankind which embodied itself in portraiture that all could appreciate. Nothing recurs more emphatically to the memory which seeks to gather up its records of her, than her vehement recoil from that spirit which identifies what is excellent with what is exceptional. The sacredness of humdrum work was one of the strongest convictions, bearing on practical life, which she ever thus expressed, and it must have been a large deduction from the happiness of her fame that it so often imposed on her (in common, we presume, with all persons of genius) the duty of checking the aspirations of that large mass of average mankind that seeks an escape from the vocation which she felt so lofty a one. The writer once felt vividly how, even among her peers, what she most valued was that which they shared with average humanity, on hearing her say of one of her few contemporaries whose genius was equal to her own, "*I* always think of him as the husband of the dead wife." The distinction of eminent powers paled, in her eyes, before that of a faithful love—profound, indeed, and deathless, but not in this respect superior to many a one that lurks behind the curtain of utter dumbness, or even of trite words and humdrum reflections. In many ways the speech recurs as eminently characteristic of her, but most of all for the precedence which it gives the ordinary human bonds beyond all that is given to the *élite* of mankind.

We pay a great tribute to any writer of such powers as hers, in saying that her teaching impresses on the mind the excellence of patient work, of simple duty, of cheerful unselfishness. In a world where restless vanity is so active, and where we are all, more or less, tempted into the scramble for pre-eminence, we owe much to one who taught us, in unforgettable words, to prize the lowly path of obscure duty. In words, we are obliged to say, for, in recalling her life, the recollection of what looks like a claim either to exceptional immunity from the laws that bind ordinary human beings, or else to an exceptional right to form a judgment on their scope, forces itself on the memory. But no plodding moralist could have more abhorred such a claim than she did. On one occasion she expressed, almost with indignation, her sense of the evil of a doctrine which compounded for moral deficiency in consideration of intellectual wealth, and her hearer failed to make her concede even that amount of truth in it which surely no deliberate view of human difficulties and limitations could ultimately withhold, and which seems to us illustrated by her own life.

From one point of view she appeared almost as the humblest of human beings. "Do not, pray, think that I would dream of comparing myself to ——," she once said, with unquestionable earnestness, mentioning an author whom most people would consider as infinitely her inferior. And the slow, careful articulation and low voice suggested, at times, something almost like diffidence. Nevertheless, mingled with this diffidence was a great consciousness of power, and one sometimes felt with her as if in the presence of royalty, while of course there were moments when one felt that exalted genius has some temptations in common with exalted rank. But they were only moments. How strong was the current of her sympathy in the direction of all humble effort, how reluctantly she checked presumption! Possibly she may sometimes have had to reproach herself with failing to check it. Surely the most ordinary and uninteresting of her friends must feel that had they known nothing of her but her rapid insight into and quick response to their inmost feelings she would still have been a memorable personality to them. This sympathy was extended to the sorrows most unlike any thing she could ever by any possibility have known; the failures of life obtained as large a share of her compassion as its sorrows.

Her aspirations to become a permanent source of joy and peace to mankind have been set forth in lines which, although they seem to us rather fine rhetoric than poetry, have already become almost classic. The wish to console and cheer was indeed rooted in the most vital part of her nature. The writer remembers her asking a person whose society gave her no pleasure, and who was not unlikely to have abused the position thus accorded, to come to her at any time that her society might be felt as consolatory, at a time of trouble. It was about the same time that she spoke of the sense of a load of possible achievement threatened by the shortening span of life with a deep sadness which in recalling the conversation seems like a prophecy. And yet none of these recollections recur to the present writer with such a rush of pathos as a few words that any one might have spoken, describing what she felt in disregarding an appeal for alms in the street.

She was much distressed, and (if the writer may judge from very slight indications) much surprised, to hear her works called depressing. She almost invariably, we believe, avoided reading any notices of them ; but her rule could not have been quite invariable, for we recall a quaint and pathetic little outburst of disappointment that the result of perusing her works should produce on some critic or other "a tendency toward black despair"—or some such expression, which, if our memory serves, she quoted with a touch of humorous exaggeration. Perhaps we shall appear merely to echo the judgment of this critic when we give it as a record of the impression she produced that one of the greatest duties of life was that of resignation. Nothing in the intercourse here recalled was more impressive as exhibiting the power of feelings to survive the convictions which gave them birth, than the earnestness with which she dwelt on this as the great and real remedy for all the ills of life. One instance in which she appeared to apply it to herself, in speaking of the short span of life that lay before her, and the large amount of achievement that must be laid aside as impossible to compress into it, has been mentioned—and the sad gentle tones in which the word *resignation* was on that occasion uttered still vibrate on the ear. Strange that it should be thought possible to transfer all that belongs to allegiance to the Will that ordains our fate except a belief in the existence of such a Will! Still more wonderful that the imagination of genius did actually achieve this transference to some extent. We regret the attempts made by some of the admirers of this noble woman to conceal, from themselves or others, the vacuum at the centre of her faith. There is this excuse for such confusion, that her works, more than any others of our day, though it is true of so many, embody the morality that centres in the faith of Christ, apart from this centre. She once said to the writer that in conversation with the narrowest and least cultivated Evangelical she could feel more sympathy than divergence; and it was impossible to doubt the fulness of meaning in her words. But there is no reason that those who reverenced her should try to veil or dilute her convictions. She made no secret of them, though the glow of feeling always hitherto associated with their opposites may have confused their outline to many of her disciples. "Deism," she once said, "seems to me the most incoherent of all systems, but to Christianity I feel no objection but its want of evidence."

Must one who feels this severance of love of man from faith in God, the great misfortune of our time, yet allow that the thing that is left acquires, for the moment, a sudden influx of new energy by the very fact of its severance? It would not be looking facts fairly in the face to deny that the genius of

George Eliot seems to show such a result. Nor is there any real difficulty in making the concession. A bud may open more quickly in water in a warm room than on its parent stem, although thus the seed will never ripen. We may transfer conviction to a more genial atmosphere at the very moment we sever it from its root, and we must wait long to discover that the life that is quickened in it is also threatened. What may be most apparent *at the moment* that faith in God expires may be the sudden release of a mystic fervor that has all to be employed in the service of man. This, we believe, is what was felt, oftenest unconsciously, in the writings of George Eliot. " What I look to," she once said, "is a time when the impulse to help our fellows shall be as immediate and as irresistible as that which I feel to grasp something firm if I am falling," and the eloquent gesture with which she grasped the mantelpiece as she spoke, remains in the memory as the expression of a sort of transmuted prayer. And now the look and the tones recur not only as one of the most valued passages in a valued chapter of memory, but as a sort of gathering up, in a noble but mutilated aspiration, of the ideal given by a lofty genius to the world.

## CHAPTER III.

### JOHN RUSKIN.

Personal appearance—His residence and surroundings—Personal eccentricities—His friendship with Carlyle.

A "STUDENT," writing to *Lippincott's Magazine* a few years ago, gives the following description of the personal appearance of the greatest art critic of our time.

Never shall I forget the first, last, and only time I ever saw John Ruskin. His picture had hung for many years just over my study-table—that sweet almost angelic face, which in somewhat coarser execution, still the same in character, fronts the title-page of some of his works. Who that has seen it has forgotten it? It is almost a child's face, and has not a little of the charm which invests one of Raphael's Sistine cherubs. But the real Ruskin, how different! I think he is the plainest man I ever saw: at any rate, no face has ever impressed me with so much ugliness. And as if to intensify nature, his manner of wearing his hair and his rude-

ly-fitting dress only emphasized the natural want of charms. Ruskin's face has neither fineness of feature nor winning expression. His eye, it is true, is large and eloquent, but not enough so to offset the rest of the face. He read a paper to a few friends that evening—not with much elegance, but with a jerky, unnatural flinging out of the words, quite unlike the flow of a good American reader. But the charm was underneath, in the thought itself, which, like every thing of Ruskin's, was original, paradoxical, stimulating. The paper was afterward printed and forms the first half of his *Sesame and Lilies*. He is a good American-hater, lives in great seclusion on Denmark Hill, one of the suburbs of London, is princely in his generosities, gracious to all young art students who seek his advice, and, with all his feudal tendencies, incontestably one of the noblest spirits of our age.

A somewhat more flattering pen-portrait is contained in this extract from *Harper's Monthly*.

### RUSKIN AT HOME.

On one of those blissful mornings which pass the year insensibly from spring to summer—beneath whose glow England expands like a water-lily on her silver seas—I sat in the study of the most eminent art critic in the world. The house is in one of the most beautiful suburbs of London, a house embowered with trees—not the mere ornamental shrubs sometimes called trees, but grand old patriarchs that had watched over the home and the grounds for a hundred years. In this mansion every thing betokened wealth, taste, and elegance. The halls ended in airy apartments, and these opened to conservatories lustrous with floral offerings from every zone, and the air was laden with breaths that told of far-off tropic affluence and the ever-burning incense of the Orient. The luminous walls and tinted ceilings combined to give the best light to the choicest works of art, gathered from every age and country. The statues looked down pure and tender, like those which, transfigured in dim remembrance, ever beckoned wandering Mignon back to her home in the South. As I waited in the library, gazing now at the pictures, and now at the fresh lawns stretching from the low windows, I seemed to be in the ideal home of a man elect by destiny to study the beautiful, and to train the eyes of the world to see it as, visibly and invisibly, it environs closely each earthly lot.

At length the man himself appeared. He was bland, affable, and kindly in manner, but still with something retractile about him, as of one over-sensitive and on guard over too quick sympathies. He had the look and voice of an idealist, but not the calmness of the optimist. He was emotional and nervous, and his voice, though rich and sweet, had a tendency to sink into a plaintive and hopeless tone. His large, light eye was soft and genial, his mouth was thin and severe. The brow was prominent, and suggested power; the chin was receding, and indicated a lack of patient endurance. I felt at once a discrepancy between the man and his home; the home meant contentment and peace —the man meant restless striving, severe discontent, ideals unfulfilled. He showed me many exquisite works of art by the greatest masters; but turned away from them, one after the other, as might Tantalus, if, while he gasped for fruits, blossoms had been set before him. And indeed I found during the conversation that it was about in this way the beautiful works struck him. He had lived among them and grown among them; they represented phases and epochs of his mental and moral history; but he had been by them trained to cravings and hopes which they could not satisfy. They too plainly heightened his ideal to a point where the earth could not fulfil it, and he stood, as it were, shivering over a lonely, unsheltered mountain peak, from which he could not descend, but which dwarfed the common world. Every beautiful work he touched corresponded with some woe that the world was suffering, as lights imply shadows. When he gazed upon some favorite picture he looked like a radiant child; another moment the picture passed, and, under some remembrance of his own or others' sorrows, he appeared to be eighty.

The conversation of this great man I refrain from repeating; the burden of it was that the art of the present day is, like its religion, imitative; a repetition of forms which once had significance and life, but now have none; a calling out of our darkness to the ancient masters, "Give us of your oil"; and that this is so because the world is too miserable, too deformed and diseased, to feed the sacred lamps of art. To build up a beautiful and characteristic art the work must not be begun with æsthetic but with moral criticism; it is not to come of taste and culture, but of political and social reform. In a word, there can be no true art where the poor have not happy homes.

In his personal characteristics Mr. Ruskin is not only one of the most whimsical, but one of the kindliest and most lovable of men. "He is idolized by his neighbors," writes a lady living in his vicinity, "we all look upon him as something even nearer than a friend,—as a loved and valued relation." He is full of benevolent crotchets. It is well known that he inherited a princely fortune, but he divided the bulk of it among his needy kinsmen, reserving to himself only £3000 a year. A large part of this sum he squanders with the idea of benefiting his fellow-man. At the time, for instance, when a great clamor was raised about adulterations in food he started a tea-store for the express purpose of supplying the British workingman with good and cheap tea. He not only lost money in the enterprise—as indeed he had expected to do—but, through the dishonesty of those he dealt with, he kept a very poor article of tea. And yet this kindly eccentric can be very bitter with his pen. Here is a sample of the sort of letters he is capable of writing to those who apply to him for intellectual assistance; in this case the answer being directed to the President of the Liberal Club at Oxford, who had been anxious to learn his views upon the political questions of the day.

MY DEAR SIR: What in the devil's name have *you* to do with either Mr. Disraeli or Mr. Gladstone? You are students at the university, and have no more business with politics than you have with rat-catching.

Had you ever read ten words of mine with understanding, you would have known that I care no more either for Mr. Disraeli or Mr. Gladstone than for two old bagpipes with the drones going by steam, but that I hate all Liberalism as I do Beelzebub, and that, with Carlyle, I stand, we two alone now in England, for God and the Queen.

Ever faithfully yours,<br>
J. RUSKIN.

The mention of Carlyle is characteristic. Ruskin's devotion to Carlyle amounts to absolute idolatry, and has been peculiarly unfortunate to himself. "The amount of nonsense," says Justin McCarthy, "that Ruskin has talked and written, under the evident conviction that thus and not otherwise would Thomas Carlyle have dealt with the subject, is something almost inconceivable. I never heard of Ruskin taking up any political question without being on the wrong side of it. I am not merely speaking of what I personally consider the wrong side; I am alluding to questions which history and hard fact and the common voice and feeling of humanity have since decided. Against every movement to give political freedom to his countrymen, against every movement to do common justice to the negro race, against every effort to secure fair play for a democratic cause, Mr. Ruskin has peremptorily arrayed himself. 'I am a Kingsman and no Mobsman,' he declares; and this declaration seems in his mind to settle the question and to justify his vindication of every despotism of caste or sovereignty. To this has his doctrine of æsthetic moral law, to this has his worship of Carlyle, conducted him."

Indeed, when a self-conceited man makes another man his idol, his very self-conceit only tends to render him more awkwardly and unconditionally servile.

A clever imitation of Carlyle's style once appeared in the public papers, in the shape of a letter upon some question of the day, purporting to be written by Carlyle himself. Out came Ruskin with another letter, in which he hailed the forgery as "not the least significant among the utterances of my Master." The ink upon Ruskin's letter was hardly dry before Carlyle issued a denunciation of the imposture and indignantly disclaimed the opinions that had been put in his mouth.

Carlyle, indeed, seemed to take not a little pleasure in publicly snubbing his erratic disciple. On another occasion Ruskin sent a letter to the papers on the subject of the alleged bad manners of the English people, as compared with those of the Continental nations; and he stated, as an illustration of this, that Carlyle could not walk out in the streets of Chelsea without being subjected to insult by the "roughs" of that region. Carlyle at once wrote to say that there was no truth in the allegation; in fact, he penned no fewer than three notes contradicting the report,—"an exhibition of candor," says the chronicler of the story, "that did not pass without comment, especially among those who could recall the time when Carlyle was wont to sally forth on horseback every Wednesday to enjoy a ride on Denmark Hill with his friend and worshipper."

In his private intercourse with his "Master," however, Ruskin was not only a tender and devoted friend, but he often exerted a beneficial influence upon the rough and rugged old Scotchman.

" He could," says G. W. Smalley, " take liberties with Carlyle which nobody else ventured upon. Everybody knows that at times Carlyle became vehement, and the conversation, if he were contradicted or argued against, was likely to be stormy. When Mrs. Carlyle was alive, she used to break in upon these scenes with the Parliamentary cry, ' Divide, Divide, Divide '— the signal for the end of a debate. I have seen

Mr. Ruskin in similar circumstances walk up to Carlyle, put his arm about his neck, and hush him tenderly to silence and calm. I hardly know whether I ought to mention such an incident, but my mention of it is, at any rate, reverent as the act was."

## CHAPTER IV.

### JOHN HENRY NEWMAN.

Cardinal Newman at Oxford—His influence over the undergraduates in his early days—His sermons at St. Mary's Church.

THE following sketch of John Henry Newman in his early days is taken from Principal Shairp's essay on Keble.

The influence he had gained, apparently without setting himself to seek it, was something altogether unlike any thing else in our time. A mysterious veneration had by degrees gathered round him, till now it was almost as though some Ambrose or Augustine of elder ages had reappeared. He himself tells how one day when he was an undergraduate, a friend with whom he was walking in the Oxford street cried out eagerly, "There's Keble!" and with what awe he looked at him. A few years, and the same took place with regard to himself. In Oriel Lane light-hearted undergraduates would drop their voices and whisper, "There's Newman!" when, head thrust forward and gaze

JOHN HENRY NEWMAN.

fixed as though on some vision seen only by himself, with swift, noiseless step he glided by. Awe fell on them for a moment almost as if it had been some apparition that had passed. For his inner circle of friends, many of them younger men, he was said to have a quite romantic affection, which they returned with the most ardent devotion and the intensest faith in him. But to the outer world he was a mystery. What were the qualities that inspired these feelings? There were, of course, learning and refinement, there was genius, not indeed of a philosopher, but of a subtle and original thinker, an unequalled edge of dialectic, and these all glorified by the imagination of a poet. Then there was the utter unworldliness, the setting at naught of all things which men most prize, the tamelessness of soul, which was ready to essay the impossible. Men felt that here was

> "One of that small transfigured band
> Which the world could not tame."

It was this mysteriousness which, beyond all his gifts of head and heart, so strangely fascinated and overawed—that something about him which made it impossible to reckon his course and take his bearing, that soul-hunger and quenchless yearning which nothing short of the eternal could satisfy. This deep and resolute ardor, this tenderness yet severity of soul, were no doubt an offense not to be forgiven by older men, especially by the wary and worldly wise; but in these lay the very spell which drew to him the hearts of all the younger and the more enthusiastic. Such was the impression he had made in Oxford just before he had relinquished his hold on it. And if at that time it seemed to persons at a distance extravagant and absurd, they may since have learned that there was in him who was the object of this reverence enough to justify it.

But, it may be asked, what actions or definite results were there to account for so deep and widespread a veneration? There were no doubt the products of his prolific pen, his works, controversial, theological, religious. But none of them were so deep in learning as some of Dr. Pusey's writings, nor so widely popular as the "Christian Year"; and yet both Dr. Pusey and Mr. Keble were at that time quite second in importance to Mr. Newman. The centre from which his power went forth was the pulpit of St. Mary's, with those wonderful afternoon sermons Sunday after Sunday, month by month, year by year, they went on, each continuing and deepening the impression the last had made. The service was very simple, no pomp, no ritualism; for it was characteristic of the leading men of the movement that they left these things to the weaker brethren. Their thoughts, at all events, were set on great questions which touched the heart of unseen things. About the service the most remarkable thing was the beauty, the silver intonation of Mr. Newman's voice as he read the Lessons. It seemed to bring new meaning out of the familiar words. Still lingers in memory the tone with which he read, "But Jerusalem which is above is free, which is the mother of us all." When he began to preach, a stranger was not likely to be much struck, especially if he had been accustomed to pulpit oratory of the Boanerges sort. Here was no vehemence, no declamation, no show of elaborated argument: so that one who came prepared to hear "a great intellectual treat" was almost sure to go away disappointed. Indeed, I believe that if he had preached one of his St. Mary's sermons before a Scotch town congregation they would have thought the preacher a "silly body." The delivery had a peculiarity which it took a new hearer some time to get over. Each separate sentence, or at least each short paragraph, was spoken rapidly, but with great clearness of intonation ; and then at its close there was a pause, lasting for nearly a half a minute; then another rapidly but clearly spoken sentence, followed by another pause. It took some time to get over this, but, that once done, the wonderful charm began to dawn on you. The look and bearing of the preacher were as of one who dwelt apart, who, though he knew his age well, did not live in it. From his seclusion of study and abstinence and prayer, from habitual dwelling in the unseen, he seemed to come forth that one day of the week to speak to others of the things he had seen and known. Those who never heard him might fancy that his sermons would generally be about apostolical succession, or rights of the Church, or against Dissenters. Nothing of the kind. You might hear him preach for weeks without an allusion to these things. What there was of High Church teaching was implied rather than enforced. The local, the temporary, and the modern were ennobled by the presence of the catholic truth belonging to all ages that pervaded the whole. His power showed itself chiefly in the new and unlooked-for way in which he touched into life old truths, moral or spiritual, which all Christians acknowledge, but most have ceased to feel. As he spoke, how the old truth became new! how it came home with a meaning never felt before! He laid his finger—how gently, yet how powerfully!—on some inner place in the hearer's heart, and told him things about himself he had never known till then. Subtlest truths which it would have taken philosophers pages of circumlocution and big words to state were dropt out by the way in a sentence or two of the most transparent Saxon. What delicacy of style, yet what calm power! how gentle, yet how strong! how simple, yet how suggestive! how homely, yet how refined! how penetrating, yet how tender-hearted! If now and then there was a forlorn undertone which at the time seemed inexplicable, if he spoke of "many a sad secret which a man dare not tell, lest he find no sympathy," of "secrets lying like cold ice upon the heart," of "some solitary, incommunicable grief," you might feel perplexed at the drift of what he spoke, but you felt all the more drawn to the speaker. To call these sermons eloquent would be no word for them ; high poems they rather were, as of an inspired singer, or the outpourings of a prophet, rapt yet self-possessed. And the tone of voice in which they were spoken, once you grew accustomed to it, sounded like a fine strain of unearthly music. Through the stillness of that high Gothic building the words fell on the ear like the measured drippings of water in some vast dim cave. After hearing these sermons you might come away still not believing the tenets peculiar to the High Church system, but you would be harder than most men if you did not feel more than ever ashamed of coarseness, selfishness, worldliness,—if you did not feel the things of faith brought closer to the soul.

## CHAPTER V.

### ALFRED TENNYSON.

*Tennyson as a recluse—His avoidance of general society—Pestered by sight-seers and photographers—Descriptions of his personal appearance by Fanny Butler and Hawthorne—A visit from Tennyson to Caroline Fox—A newspaper Mosaic.*

THERE is no public man of our day whose private life has been kept so sacredly shrouded from the vulgar gaze as that of Tennyson. His studies, his tastes, and something of his personal character may indeed be traced in his writings,—with an essentially lyrical poet who sings out of a full heart it could not well be otherwise,—but his history evades us. He has been largely written about by those who know him, but they have conspicuously omitted to tell us any thing about him. He figures in Horne's " Spirit of the Age " (published in 1844),—and the express purpose of that book was to give some insight into the private as well as the public life of the noted men of the day,—but, with twenty pages of criticism on the poet, these dozen lines are all that relate to the man:

"He has brothers and sisters living, who are all possessed of superior attainments. Avoiding general society, he would prefer to sit up all night talking with a friend, or else to sit 'and think alone.' Beyond a very small circle he is never to be met. There is nothing eventful in his biography, of a kind which would interest the public; and, wishing to respect the retirement he unaffectedly desires, we close the present paper."

Even that inveterate bookmaker, William Howitt, in his "Homes and Haunts of the Poets," confesses himself baffled by this determined privacy. "Alfred Tennyson," he says, "moves on his way through life heard but by the public unseen. We might put to him a question similar to that which Wordsworth put to the cuckoo, and our question would have like answer. Many an admiring man may have said with Solomon of old, 'I have sought him, but I could not find him; I called him, but he answered not.'" Howitt gives the following as the substance of all that he has been able to learn about Tennyson: "I believe he has spent some years in London, and he may be traced to Hastings, Eastbourne, Cheltenham, the Isle of Wight, and the like places. It is very possible you may come across him in a country inn, with a foot on each hob of the fireplace, a volume of Greek in one hand, his meerschaum in the other, so far advanced toward the seventh heaven that he would not thank you to call him back into this nether world. Wherever he is, however, in some still nook of enormous London, or the stiller one of some far-off sea-side hamlet, he is pondering a lay for eternity:

> Losing his fine and active might
> In a silent meditation,
> Falling into a still delight
> And luxury of contemplation.

"That luxury shall, one day, be mine and yours, transferred to us in the shape of a third volume: so come away and don't disturb him."

This very isolation of Tennyson's has whetted curiosity to an intense degree. No house has been so besieged by tourists as his Isle of Wight residence. A few years ago a paragraph went the rounds of the press describing what he had to suffer at the hands of these creatures. He was obliged to build a high wall about his grounds, with locked gates, to keep curious people away. The locked-out crowd, we are told, prowl outside, and climb up and look over, There is a row of heads all around the wall. When Tennyson comes out to walk in his garden the crowd rushes frantically to the side where he is. Photographers stand ready at all angles to catch pictures of him. Some of them have made holes in the wall and inserted the tubes of the cameras therein, where they remain stationary, their owners hoping and watching for a chance to take the poet's picture. When he is discovered, the cameras are put in residence and the photographers take aim, happy if they secure a glimpse of the corner of his cloak or a rear view of him bending to smell a violet in its bed. He looks despairingly at the heads, he frowns at them in vain. They stare, they make audible comments about him. "Why does he stand there like a post?" says one.—"Like a Stoughton bottle," says another.—"What queer buttons he has!"—"And where could he have found that cloak?" say they. They bring their dinners and lie in wait for him. The land around is trampled, the grass is killed, and the earth is strewn with dinner-papers, crusts, and empty beer-bottles. A path lies around the walls, trodden hard as adamant.

Fanny Kemble has a brief allusion, in her "Records of a Girlhood," to an evening spent with Tennyson. She confesses herself a little disappointed with the exterior of the poet "in spite of his eyes, which are very fine; his head and face, striking and dignified as they are, are almost too ponderous and massive for beauty in so young a man; and every now and then there is a slight sarcastic expression about his mouth that almost frightens me, in spite of his shy manner and habitual silence. But, after all, it is delightful to see and be with any one that one admires and loves for what he has done, as I do him."

This was in 1832. Twenty-two years later, in a ramble through the Manchester Exhibition Rooms, Hawthorne saw Tennyson in his serene and cheerful maturity. "Gazing at him with all my eyes," says the American romancer in his "Note-Books," "I liked him well, and rejoiced more in him than in all the other wonders of the Exhibition. * * * He is as un-English as possible; indeed, an Englishman of genius usually lacks the national characteristics and is great abnormally. Un-English as he was, Tennyson had not, however, an American look. I cannot well describe the difference, but there was something more mellow in him—softer, sweeter, broader, more simple than we are apt to be. Living apart from men, as he does, would hurt any one of us more than it does him. I may as well leave him here, for I cannot touch the central point." When Mr. Fields some years afterward told Tennyson, who was then engaged in reading the "Twice-Told Tales," that Hawthorne had seen him at Manchester, but did not make himself known, the Laureate said, in his frank and hearty manner, "Why did n't he come up and let me shake hands with him? I am sure I would have been glad to meet a man like Hawthorne anywhere."

In Caroline Fox's recently published "Memories of Old Friends," I find the following account of

A VISIT FROM TENNYSON.

*Falmouth, September* 22, 1866.—When Alfred Tennyson and his friend Francis Palgrave were at Falmouth, they made inquiries about the Grove Hill\*

---

\* Supposed to be an original sketch for the picture of the Last Supper, by Leonardo da Vinci, and now in the possession of Robert Fox at Falmouth.

Leonardo, so of course we asked them to come and see it; and thus we had a visit of two glorious hours both here and in the other garden. As Tennyson has a perfect horror of being lionized, we left him very much to himself for a while, till he took the initiative and came forth. *Apropos* of the Leonardo, he said that the head of Christ in the Raising of Lazarus was to his mind the worthiest representation of the subject which he had ever seen. His bright, thoughtful friend, Francis Palgrave, was the more fond of pictures of the two: they both delighted in the little Cuyp and the great Correggio; thought the Guido a pleasant thing to have, though feeble enough; believed in the Leonardo; and Palgrave gloated over the big vase. On the leads we were all very happy and talked apace. "The great T." groaned a little over the lionizing to which he is subject, and wondered how it came out at Falmouth that he was here: this was *apropos* of my speaking of Henry Hallam's story of a miner hiding behind a wall to look at him, which he did not remember; but when he heard the name of Hallam, how his great gray eyes opened, and gave one a moment's glimpse into the depths in which "In Memoriam" learned its infinite wail. He talked a good deal of his former visit to Cornwall, and his accident at Bude, all owing to a stupid servant-maid. In the garden he was greatly interested, for he, too, is trying to acclimatize plants, but finds us far ahead, because he is at the western extremity of the Isle of Wight, where the keen winds cut up their trees and scare away the nightingales in consequence. But he is proud and happy in a great magnolia in his garden. He talked of the Cornish, and rather liked the conceit of their countryism; was amused to hear of the refractory Truro clergyman being buried by the Cornish miners, whom he forbade to sing at their own funeral; but he thought it rather an unfortunate instance of the civilizing power of Wesley. By degrees we got to Guinevere, and he spoke kindly of S. Hodges' picture of her at the Polytechnic, though he doubted if it told the story very distinctly. This led to real talk of Arthur and the "Idyls," and his firm belief in him as an historical personage, though old Speed's narrative has much that can be only traditional. He found great difficulty in reconstructing the character, in connecting modern with ancient feeling in representing the ideal king. I asked whether Vivien might not be the old Brittany fairy who wiled Merlin into her net, and not an actual woman. "But no," he said; "it is full of distinct personality, though I never expect women to like it." The river Camel he well believes in, particularly as he slipped his foot and fell in the other day, but found no Excalibur. Camel means simply winding, crooked, like the Cam at Cambridge. The Welsh claim Arthur as their own, but Tennyson gives all his votes to us. Some have urged him to continue the "Idyls," but he does not feel it expedient to take people's advice as an absolute law, but to wait for the vision. He reads the reviews of his poems, and is amused to find how often he is misunderstood. Poets often misinterpret poets, and he has never seen an artist truly illustrate a poet. Talked of Garibaldi, whose life was like one out of Plutarch, he said, so grand and simple; and of Ruskin, as one who has said many foolish things; and of John Sterling, whom he met twice, and whose conversational powers he well remembers.

Tennyson is a grand specimen of a man, with a magnificent head set on his shoulders like the capital of a mighty pillar. His hair is long and wavy and covers a massive head. He wears a beard and moustache, which one begrudges as hiding so much of that firm, powerful, but finely chiselled mouth. His eyes are large and gray, and open wide when a subject interests him; they are well shaded by the noble brow, with its strong lines of thought and suffering. I can quite understand Samuel Laurence calling it the best balance of head he had ever seen.

These excerpts represent about all the references to Tennyson which are to be found in contemporary volumes of biography or remniscence. But since the advent of the professional "interviewer," a number of paragraphs regarding the poet have been set floating through the daily press, and from these sources I have constructed the following mosaic, which, while it does not rise to the dignity of a "pen picture," at least contains some information in regard to the habits and personal peculiarities of the Laureate.

SOME JOURNALISTIC TENNYSONIANA.

Tennyson's manner [we are told] has a brusqueness and bluntness about it which is at first rather startling to one who has only known him through his books. He utters his opinions in a plain, straightforward way, choosing the homeliest Saxon words and rarely rising to any thing like the heroic strain. His disregard of the conventionalities of life is, however, thoroughly natural and unaffected. "His customary suit of light gray, hanging about him in many a fold, like the hide of a rhinoceros, the loose, ill-fitting collar and carelessly knotted tie, the wide, low boots, are not worn, you may be sure, for artistic effect, or with the foppishness of a Byron." He is an inveterate smoker. Poet and dweller in the empyrean though he be, he knows nothing of Ruskin's scorn for those who "pollute the pure air of morning with cigar smoke." But he does not affect the mild Havana in any of its varied forms. A brother poet who spent a week with him at his country-seat says that Partagas,

Regalias, and Cabanas have no charm for him. He prefers a pipe, and of all pipes in the world the common clay pipe is his choice. His den is at the top of the house. When he sits down to work in the morning a huge tobacco-jar, big enough for an ancestral urn, is at his feet, together with a box full of white clay pipes. Filling one of these, he smokes until it is empty, breaks it in twain, and throws the fragments into another box prepared for their reception. Then he pulls out a fresh pipe, fills it, smokes it, and destroys it as before. He will not smoke a pipe the second time. While at work he allows no one to disturb him, unless upon an errand of life or death; but as soon as his morning's labors are over he is glad to see his friends, sends for them, indeed, if they be in the house, or announces by a little bell his readiness to receive them. But his chief delight is not in communion with his fellows. Rather is it to lounge at the window of his study, surrounded by a few choice books of favorite authors, and in full view of the magnificent island scenery, with the gray line of undulating hills and the streak of silver sea in the distance. At other times he will wander down to the zigzag pathways that meander in all directions through the tall hazel twigs which hem his house around, where one comes suddenly on a little secluded dale bright with mossy verdure, or a garden laden with odors from a score of pine-trees, or a bigger lawn devoted to the innocent pursuit of croquet or lawn-tennis. Less frequently he may be seen walking through the neighboring byways and exciting the curiosity of the village folks by the strangeness of his mien and the eccentricity of his costume. In all his out-of-door excursions he is sure to be accompanied by one or other of his handsome sons, "full-limbed and tall." She, the "dear, near and true," whose sweet faith in him was ever the incentive to greater labor and higher aspirations, is no longer able to be by his side in work; but invalid as she is, she still finds opportunity for ministering to the wants of the poor about her gates.

## CHAPTER VI.

### RALPH WALDO EMERSON.

Emerson as a lecturer, by N. P. Willis—Miss Bremer's visit to the Emerson household—Hawthorne's account of Emerson and his admirers.

OF Mr. Emerson's personal appearance upon the platform in the old days when he was one of the most popular of lecturers, the gossipy N. P. Willis has given us an off-hand sketch which is interesting enough to quote.

#### EMERSON AS A LECTURER.

The single look we were enabled to give Mr. Emerson, as the applause announced that he had come into the pulpit, revealed to us that he was a man we had seen a thousand times, and with whose face our memory was familiar; though in the sidewalk portrait-taking by which we had treasured his physiognomy there was so little resemblance to the portrait taken from reading him, that we should never have put the two together, probably, except by personal identification. We remember him perfectly as a boy whom we used to see playing about Chauncey Place and Summer Street,—one of those pale little moral-sublimes with their shirt-collars turned over, who are recognized by Boston schoolboys as having " fathers that are Unitarians,"—and, though he came to his first short hair about the time that we came to our first tail-coat, six or eight years behind us, we have never lost sight of him. In the visits we have made to Boston of late years, we have seen him in the street and remembered having always seen him as a boy—very little suspecting that *there* walked, in a form long familiar, the deity of an intellectual altar upon which, at that moment, burned a fire in our bosom.

Emerson's voice is up to his reputation. It has a curious contradiction, which we tried in vain to analyze satisfactorily,—an outwardly repellent and inwardly reverential mingling of qualities which a musical composer would despair of blending into one. It bespeaks a life that is half contempt, half adoring recognition, and very little between. But it is noble altogether. And what seems strange is to hear such a voice proceeding from such a body. It is a voice with shoulders in it which he has not —with lungs in it far larger than his—with a walk in it which the public never see—with a fist in it which his own hand never gave him the model for —and with a gentleman in it which his parochial and "bare-necessaries-of-life" sort of exterior give no other betrayal of. We can imagine nothing in nature (which seems, too, to have a type for every thing) like the want of correspondence between the Emerson that goes in at the eye and the Emerson that goes in at the ear. We speak without having had an opportunity to study his face,— acquaintance with features, as everybody knows, being like the peeling of an artichoke, and the *core* of a face, to those who know it, being very unlike the eight or ten outside folds that stop the eye in the beginning. But a heavy and vase-like blossom of a magnolia, with fragrance enough to perfume a whole wilderness, which should be lifted by a whirlwind and dropped into a branch of an aspen, would not seem more as if it never could have grown there, than Emerson's voice seems inspired and foreign to his visible and natural body. Indeed (to use one of his own similitudes), his body seems "never to have broken the umbilical cord" which held it to Boston, while his soul has sprung to the adult stature of a child of the universe, and his voice is the utterance of the soul only. It is one of his fine remarks, that "it makes a great difference to the force of any sentence whether a man is behind it or no"; but without his voice to make the ear stand surety for his value, the eye would look for the first time on Emerson and protest his draft on admiration, as *not* "payable at sight."

This is essentially what Carlyle would have called the "flunky" view of Emerson, particularly in the denial to the stately and noble-looking philosopher of the outward characteristics of a gentleman. The gentlemanly characteristics, in Mr. Willis' eye, were those externals which result from the combined efforts of that noble triumvirate, the tailor, the hair-dresser, and the dancing-master. It is pleasant, therefore, to turn to another chronicler, who, although she confesses herself baffled in her attempt to reach the inner penetralia of Emerson's mind, still has a deep and even awed appreciation of some of his finest traits. Miss Frederika Bremer in her visit to the United States was thrown into frequent contact with the Concord sage, and she thus jots down her impressions in her home-bound letters.

### MISS BREMER'S VISITS TO EMERSON.

*December* 2, 1849.—Emerson came to meet us, walking down the little avenue of spruce firs which leads from his house, bareheaded amid the falling snow. He is a quiet, nobly grave figure, his complexion pale, with strongly marked features and dark hair. He seemed to me a younger man, but less handsome, than I had imagined ; his exterior not so fascinating, but more significant. He occupied himself with us, however, and with me in particular, as a lady and a foreigner, kindly and agreeably. He is a very peculiar character, but too cold and hypercritical to please me entirely ; a strong clear eye, always looking out for an ideal which he never finds realized on earth ; discovering wants, shortcomings, imperfections ; and too strong and healthy himself to understand other people's weaknesses and sufferings, for he even despises suffering as a weakness unworthy of higher natures. This singularity of character leads one to suppose that he has never been ill ; sorrows, however, he has had, and has felt them deeply, as some of his most beautiful poems prove ; nevertheless, he has only allowed himself to be bowed for a short time by these griefs,—the death of two beautiful and beloved brothers, as well as of a beautiful little boy, his eldest son. He has also lost his first wife, after having been married scarcely a year.

Emerson is now married for the second time, and has three children. His pretty little boy, the youngest of his children, seems to be, in particular, dear to him. Mrs. Emerson has beautiful eyes, full of feeling, but she appears delicate, and is in character very different from her husband. He interested me without warming me. That critical crystalline and cold nature may be very estimable, quite healthy, and, in its way, beneficial for those who possess it, and also for others who allow themselves to be measured and criticised by it; but for me —David's heart with David's songs!

I shall return to this home in consequence of a very kind invitation to do so from Emerson and his wife, and in order that I may see more of this sphinx-like individual.

*January* 22, 1850.—I must now tell you about Concord and the sphinx in Concord, Waldo Emerson, because I went to Concord five days ago, attended by—himself. During the four days that I remained in Emerson's house I had a real enjoyment in the study of this strong, noble, eagle-like nature. Any near approximation was, as it were, imperfect, because our characters and views are fundamentally dissimilar, and that secret antagonism which exists in me toward him, spite of my admiration, would at times awake, and this easily called forth his icy-alp nature, repulsive and chilling. But this is not the original nature of the man; he does not rightly thrive in it, and he gladly throws it off, if he can, and is much happier, as one can see, in a mild and sunny atmosphere, where the natural beauty of his being may breathe freely and expand into blossom, touched by that of others as by a living breeze. I enjoyed the contemplation of him in his demeanor, his expression, his mode of talking, and his every-day life, as I enjoy contemplating the calm flow of a river bearing along, and between flowery shores, large and small vessels—as I love to see the eagle circling in the clouds, resting upon them and its pinions. In this calm elevation Emerson allows nothing to reach him, neither great nor small, neither prosperity nor adversity.

Pantheistic as Emerson is in his philosophy, in the moral view with which he regards the world and life he is in a high degree pure, noble, and severe, demanding as much from himself as he demands from others. His words are severe, his judgment often keen and merciless, but his demeanor is alike noble and pleasing, and his voice beautiful. One may quarrel with Emerson's thoughts, with his judgment, but not with himself. That which struck me most, as distinguishing him from most other human beings, is *nobility*. He is a born nobleman. I have seen before two other men born with this stamp upon them. Emerson is the third who has it, and perhaps in a yet higher degree. And added thereto that deep intonation of voice, that expression, so mild yet so elevated at the same time. I could not but think of Maria Lowell's words, "If he merely mentions my name I feel myself ennobled."

I said to an amiable woman, a sincere friend of Emerson's, and one who, at the same time, is possessed of a deeply religious mind, "How can you love him so deeply, when he does not love nor put faith in the Highest, which we love?"

"He is so faultless," replied she; "and then he is lovely!"

Lovable he is, also, as one sees him in his home and amid his domestic relations. But you shall hear more about him when we meet, and you shall see his strong beautiful head in my album, among many American acquaintance. I feel that my intercourse with him will leave a deep trace on my soul.

Better than either of the above, however, because from the pen of a deeper thinker and a broader-minded man, is the following description of Emerson in Hawthorne's "Mosses from an Old Manse."

### HAWTHORNE'S DESCRIPTION OF EMERSON.

Were I to adopt a pet theory, as so many people do, and fondle it in my embraces to the exclusion of all others, it would be that the great want which mankind labors under at this present period is sleep. The world should recline its vast head on the first convenient pillow, and take an age-long nap. It has gone distracted through a morbid activity, and, while preternaturally wide awake, is nevertheless tormented by visions which seem real to it now, but would assume their true aspect and character were all things once set right by an interval of sound repose. This is the only method of getting rid of old delusions and avoiding new ones; of regenerating our race, so that it might in due time awake as an infant out of dewy slumber; of restoring to us the simple perception of what is right, and the single-hearted desire to achieve it, both of which have long been lost in consequence of this weary activity of brain and torpor or passion of the heart that now afflict the universe. Stimulants, the only mode of treatment hitherto attempted, cannot quell the disease; they do but heighten the delirium.

Let not the above paragraph ever be quoted against the author; for, though tinctured with its modicum of truth, it is the result and expression of what he knew, while he was writing, to be but a distorted survey of the state and prospects of mankind. There were circumstances around me which made it difficult to view the world precisely as it exists; for, severe and sober as was the Old Manse, it was necessary to go but a little beyond its threshold before meeting with stranger moral shapes of men than might have been encountered elsewhere in a circuit of a thousand miles.

These hobgoblins of flesh and blood were attracted thither by the wide-spreading influence of a great original thinker, who had his earthly abode at the opposite extremity of our village. His mind acted upon other minds of a certain constitution with wonderful magnetism, and drew many men upon long pilgrimages to speak with him face to face. Young visionaries—to whom just so much of insight had been imparted as to make life all a labyrinth around them—came to seek the clew that should guide them out of their self-involved bewilderment. Gray-headed theorists—whose systems, at first air, had finally imprisoned them in an iron framework—travelled painfully to his door, not to ask deliverance, but to invite the free spirit into their own thraldom. People that had lighted upon a new thought, or a thought that they fancied new, came to Emerson, as the finder of a glittering gem hastens to a lapidary, to ascertain its quality and value. Uncertain, troubled, earnest wanderers through the midnight of the moral world beheld his intellectual fire as a beacon burning on a hilltop, and, climbing the difficult ascent, looked forth into the surrounding obscurity more hopefully than hitherto. The light revealed objects unseen before —mountains, gleaming lakes, glimpses of a creation among the chaos; but also, as was unavoidable, it attracted bats and owls and the whole host of night-birds, which flapped their dusky wings against the gazer's eyes, and sometimes were mistaken for fowls of angelic feather. Such delusions always hover nigh whenever a beacon-fire of truth is kindled.

For myself, there had been epochs of my life when I, too, might have asked of this prophet the master-word that should solve me the riddle of the universe, but now, being happy, I felt that there were no questions to be put, and therefore admired Emerson as a poet of deep beauty and austere tenderness, but sought nothing from him as a philosopher. It was good, nevertheless, to meet him in the wood-paths, or sometimes in our avenue, with that pure intellectual gleam diffused about his presence like the garment of a shining one ; and he so quiet, so simple, so without pretension, encountering each man alive, as if expecting to receive more than he could impart. And, in truth, the heart of many an ordinary man has, perchance, inscriptions which he could not read. But it was impossible to dwell in his vicinity without inhaling more or less the mountain atmosphere of his lofty thought, which, in the brains of some people, wrought a singular giddiness—new truth being as heavy as new wine. Never was a poor little country village infested with such a variety of queer, strangely dressed, oddly behaved mortals, most of whom took it upon themselves to be important agents of the world's destiny, yet were simply bores of a very intense water. Such, I imagine, is the invariable character of persons who crowd so closely upon an original thinker as to draw in his unuttered breath and thus become imbued with a false originality. This triteness of novelty is enough to make any man of common sense blaspheme at all ideas of less than a century's standing, and pray that the world may be petrified and rendered immovable in precisely the worst moral and physical state that it ever yet arrived at, rather than be benefited by such schemes of such philosophers.

## CHAPTER VII.

### WILLIAM CULLEN BRYANT.

*A conversation with Bryant by Mrs. Elizabeth Oakes Smith—Hawthorne's record of a visit from Bryant—Various anecdotes—John Bigelow's reminiscences.*

"It is a fine sight," says Mrs. Elizabeth Oakes Smith in an old number of *Appleton's Monthly*, "a man full of years, clear in mind, sober in judgment, refined in taste, and handsome in person. Such is Mr. Bryant, Nestor among the poets, who has not yet survived his fame—hardly ever received, as yet, his full meed of praise. I remember once to have been at a lecture where Mr. Bryant sat several seats in front of me, and his finely-shaped and ample-sized head was especially noticeable, even compared with the mass of intelligent heads by which he was surrounded. Heads grow to a late period in life, unless people dwindle, peak, and pine, and stint themselves by frivolous or unworthy habits or pursuits.

The observer of Bryant's capacious skull and most refined expression of face cannot fail to read therein the history of a noble manhood."

Mrs. Smith then goes on to give the following record of

### A CONVERSATION WITH BRYANT.

There is that in the most ordinary utterances of genius that fixes itself upon the mind, and will not be erased ; and men of genius talk at a sort of peril. I believe I can recall every word of the conversations of Mr. Bryant with me, and I do not believe he ever uttered one that ought to be forgotten. He is by no means a loquacious man,—his paragraphs are all fastidiously finished, and would read well in print. He is apt to be electric in society, and talks with those whom he most fancies, who are sure to be unpretentious, real, and distinctive in character.

"How is it you can make Mr. Bryant talk?" asked Mrs. E—— one evening.

"Simply by not trying to be smart, and making no effort to talk well," was the reply.

Margaret Fuller, Mr. Bryant, and many others, were at a party at Marcus and Rebecca Spring's, whose genial hospitality made their home a favorite place of resort. It was a chill November evening, and, as the wind scattered the foliage against the lattice, Mrs. E—— repeated, looking at Mr. Bryant:

> " The melancholy days are come,
> The saddest of the year."

Mr. Bryant bowed slightly, and she passed on ; when the former turned his dark eyes full upon me, and said, in his most cold and quiet manner:

"It is enough to make an author distrust his own productions to hear one, not by any means his best, quoted at the expense of all others."

"I should not think so ; it only proves that the one in question has touched the common thought, while his other productions may be beyond it."

"That is a pleasant view most certainly, but still the doubt remains."

"I should not think the author of 'Thanatopsis' would be troubled with many doubts."

"Ah! there the same doubt recurs. A poem written so early in life, and quoted, as you do now, as an author's best, leaves a doubt of mental progress, painful to reflect upon."

This was said with more feeling than I had anticipated from that ordinarily undemonstrative speaker. One might have supposed it akin to those courteous tactics by which accomplished men, to use a vulgar phrase, "fish for a compliment" from a woman known to be no flatterer, and not incapable of judgment ; but Mr. Bryant is not in the least vain, and has a manly appreciation of his own abilities. I replied :

"I do not quite see the subject in the light you place it. A poet, if truly such, must have his hours of inspiration, when his thought and expression transcend himself, and utter at a breath what it will take him years to reach by any deliberate mental process."

Mr. Bryant's fine eyes kindled as he replied : "That is a pleasant solution, and the poet ought to be reconciled."

Mr. Bryant is tall and slender, his general appearance indicating high and refined nervous action. His well-shaped head is covered with soft, wavy hair, which is now of a silvery whiteness.

In his Italian Note-Books, Hawthorne makes record of a visit paid him by Bryant in Florence.

### HAWTHORNE'S SKETCH OF BRYANT.

I never saw him but once before [says Hawthorne], and that was at the door of our little red cottage in Lenox ; he sitting in a wagon with one or two of the Sedgwicks, merely exchanging a greeting with me from under the brim of his straw hat, and driving on. He presented himself now with a long white beard, such as a palmer might have worn as the growth of his long pilgrimages ; a brow almost

entirely bald, and what hair he had quite heavy;
a forehead impending, yet not massive ; dark bushy
eyebrows, and keen eyes, without much softness in
them; a dark and sallow complexion; a slender figure,
bent a little with age, but at once alert and infirm.
It surprised me to see him so venerable, for as poets
are Apollo's kinsmen, we are inclined to attribute to
them his enviable quality of never growing old.
There was a weary look in his face, as if he were
tired of seeing things and doing things, though with
certainly enough still to see and do, if need were.
My family gathered about him, and he conversed
with great readiness and simplicity about his travels,
and whatever other subject came up ; telling us that
he had been abroad five times, and was now getting
a little homesick, and had no more eagerness for
sights, though his "gals." (as he called his daughters and another young lady) dragged him out to
see the wonders of Rome again. His manners and
whole aspect are very particularly plain, though not
affectedly so ; but it seems as if in the decline of
life and the security of his position he had put off
whatever artificial polish he may have heretofore had,
and resumed the simpler habits and deportment of
his early New England breeding. Not but what
you discover, nevertheless, that he is a man of refinement, who has seen the world and is well aware
of his own place in it. He uttered neither passion
nor poetry, but excellent good sense, and accurate

information on whatever subject transpired ; a very pleasant man to associate with, but rather cold, I should imagine if one should seek to touch his heart with one's own. He shook hands kindly all round, but not with any warmth of grip ; although the ease of his deportment had put us all on sociable terms with him.

Since the death of Bryant a number of his acquaintances have given us their reminiscences of the poet, which seem to confirm the impression he made upon Hawthorne. His manner was one of unfailing kindness and courtesy, his relations with those around him were of the pleasantest description, but he was of too reserved a nature for any intimate companionship. Still, his reserve, we are told, was rather that of shy modesty than of conscious worth. His intercourse with his associates in the office of the *Evening Post* was always singularly frank and easy. He even avoided that appearance of superior authority which is almost inseparable from the exercise of control over the working of a newspaper staff. His few and infrequent commands were requests always, framed in the language and uttered in the tone of one who asks a favor, not of one who merely wishes to disguise a command.

Notwithstanding his age and his chiefship in the office, he never sent for any member of his staff to come to him; if he had aught to say he went to the person to whom he wished to say it. "He would pass through the editorial rooms with a cheery 'good morning'; he would sit down by one's desk and talk if there was aught to talk about; or, if asked a question while passing, would stand while answering it, and frequently would relate some anecdote suggested by the question, or offer some apt quotation to illustrate the subject under discussion." His tenderness of the feelings of others and his earnest desire always to avoid the giving of unnecessary pain, were very marked. "Soon after I began to do the duties of literary editor," continues an associate, "Mr. Bryant, who was reading a review of a little book of wretchedly halting verse, said to me: 'I wish you would deal very gently with poets, especially the weaker ones.' Later, I had a very bad case of poetic idiocy to deal with, and as Mr. Bryant happened to come into my room while I was debating the matter in my mind, I said to him that I was embarrassed by his injunction to deal gently with poets, and pointed out to him the utter impossibility of finding any thing to praise or lightly to condemn in the book before me. After I had read some of its stanzas to him, he answered: ' No, you can't praise it, of course; it won't do to lie about it, but '—turning the volume in his hand and inspecting it—' you might say that the binding is securely put on, and that—well, the binder has planed the edges pretty smooth.' "

In an address delivered before the Century Club, the Hon. John Bigelow, who was a personal friend of the poet, gives the following

### REMINISCENCES OF BRYANT.

Plutarch tells us of a Roman judge refusing to act upon the testimony of a single witness in a case where the law required the testimony of two witnesses. "No," said the judge, "not even if Cato himself were the witness." This country has probably produced no person to whose truthfulness a similar homage from the bench would seem less inappropriate than to Bryant. A statement from him required no sanction. His profound conscientiousness, too, invested his character with an atmosphere in which no unworthy or degrading purpose could breathe or exist for a moment. And here lay the secret of a personal dignity which with him was more than majestic. Though with his friends one of the most genial and to all the world the most unpretending of men, one would as soon think of taking a liberty with the Pope as with Bryant.

The impression he left upon strangers when first presented to him was apt to be chilling. Though never unkind, his manner in such cases was not responsive. His greetings were discouraging, especially to the numbers whose admiration for him had been feeding for years upon an ideal shaped from his works, and who regarded an introduction to him as an epoch in their lives. This apparent want of cordiality did not result from insensibility, nor wholly from his constitutional aversion to be lionized, but rather from an unwillingness to express in any way a greater degree of interest than he felt. As soon as acquaintance ripened a feeling of greater cordiality, his manner betrayed it, but always within the limits of the strictest truthfulness. He spoke and lived

> " As ever in his great Taskmaster's eye,"

and expecting to account for every word he uttered.

Whoever will adopt the same lofty rule in his intercourse with the world, will soon find the true explanation of much that in Bryant was attributed to a cold and unsympathetic treatment. He took little note of any but moral distinctions among men. Mere worldly rank impressed him less than almost any man I ever knew. I was once his guest at Roslyn with a foreigner of some distinction, who at the close of the first repast after our arrival, presumed upon the privilege accorded to persons of his rank at home to rise first and dismiss the table. Mr. Bryant joined me on our way to the parlor, and with an expression of undisguised astonishment asked me, "Did you see that?" I replied that I did, and with a view of extenuating the gentleman's offense as much as I could, said that he evidently thought he only was exercising one of the recognized prerogatives of his order. "Well," he said, "he will have no opportunity of repeating it here"; and he was as good as his word, for during the remainder of our sojourn, no one was left in doubt whose prerogative it was in that house to dismiss the table. Some weeks later he alluded to this incident and quoted, from a conversation he had once held with Fenimore Cooper, his strictures upon this exasperating assumption of the titled classes in some communities of the Old World. He was willing that others should adopt any standard that pleased them best, by which to rate their fellows, himself included, but he would not accept directly or indirectly for himself any other standard than that which, so far as he knew, his Maker would apply.

As Bryant, from the day he embarked in journalism, continued a journalist until the close of his life, from a yet earlier period of his life to its close he never ceased to be a poet; reminding us of Cowley's remark that it is seldom seen that the poet dies before the man. But Bryant never confounded the two vocations in any way, or allowed either to interfere to any appreciable extent with the other. They constituted two separate and distinct currents of intellectual life, one running through the other if you please, but never mixing with it, as the Gulf Stream winds its way through the broad Atlantic, though always distinguished from it by its higher temperature. None of the more vulgar considerations of authorship ever operated upon his muse so far as I was ever able to discern. He never sang for money ; neither did he use his poetical gifts for worldly or professional ends. He used his feet for walking and he used his wings for flying, but he never attempted to fly with his feet or to run with his wings. He earned his bread and he fought the battle of life with his journal, but he made no secret of the fact that he looked to his verses for the perpetuation of his name ; when he put on his singing robes he practically withdrew from the world and went up into a high mountain, where the din and clamor of professional life, in which he habitually dwelt, was inaudible. On those occasions

"His soul was like a star, and dwelt apart."

When the semi-centennial anniversary of the *Evening Post* was approaching, I proposed to him to prepare for its columns a sketch of its career.

He cheerfully accepted the task, and in order that he might be free from interruption, I recommended him to go down to his country-home at Roslyn and remain there until it was finished, and let me send him there such of the files of the paper as he might have occasion to consult. He rejected the proposal as abruptly as if I had asked him to offer sacrifices to Apollo. He would allow no such work to follow him there. Not even the shadow of his business must fall upon the consecrated haunts of his muse. He rarely brought or sent any thing from the country for the *Evening Post;* but if he did, it was easy to detect in the character of the fish that they had been caught in strange waters. This separation of his professional from his poetical life must be taken into account in any effort to explain the uniform esteem in which he was always held as a poet by his country-people, while, not unfrequently, one of the least popular of journalists. I have heard his verses quoted in public meetings, during the earlier stages of the anti-slavery controversy, where if he had appeared in person he could have scarcely escaped outrage. No poet of eminence probably had less of the benefit of adverse criticism, while as a journalist he was almost always embattled.

I once asked him how it happened that in a profession generally so fatal to the higher qualities of style, because of the haste in which much of its work has to be done, he had managed for more than half a century to preserve his style in such purity and perfection. "If my style has fewer defects than you expect," he said, "it is for the reason, I suppose, which Dr. Johnson gave Boswell for conversing so well: I always write my best." "But," I said, "there are daily emergencies when there is no time to choose words and be dainty, when the alternative is a hasty article or none at all." "I would sooner the paper would go to press without an editorial article than send to the printer one I was not satisfied with," was his reply.

Pope excused himself to one of his correspondents for neglect of style and method in his familiar letters, on the ground that he was writing to a friend. I will venture to say that Bryant never offered or needed any such excuse for himself, and that he never wrote a note to his grocer or butcher that, in so far as its form and expression were concerned, was not as faultless as if it had been written for the press.

Dr. Johnson makes it a reproach to Pope that he wrote his translation of the Iliad upon the backs of old letters. Mr. Bryant rarely wrote for the *Evening Post* upon any thing else, not, as Johnson intimated in the case of Pope, from a penny-wise and pound-foolish parsimony, but from a principle which was one of the logical consequences of his theory of human responsibility. His table was filled with old letters on their way to the paper-mill. They were as serviceable for his editorial work as if they were fresh from it. He used them because he believed that everybody in the world was made the poorer by every thing that is wasted, and no one so much as he who wastes, for he experiences a waste of character as well as of property.

It could be said of Bryant, if of any man, that he had no vices. Neither had he any time-wasting habits. He never consciously indulged any appetite or taste to the prejudice of his health or of any duty. Without being in the least an ascetic, or foregoing any of the legitimate pleasures of the table, he had occasion to lose no time in repairing forces exhausted by any species of excess. I could not conceive of his indulging in any thing which he even suspected might impair his mental, moral, or physical efficiency, merely because it gave a transient gratification. He never seemed to exercise self-denial, so completely had it become the law of his life to do what appeared to him best to be done. This was the secret of his almost miraculous health, which preserved him in the full enjoyment of all his faculties up to his last illness, and which enabled him, after he was seventy years of age, to associate his name imperishably with the greatest of epic poets, by the least imperfect English translation of the Iliad and Odyssey that has yet been made.

I am warranted in saying that, until the distressing accident which terminated his days, he was never disabled by sickness within the memory of any person now living.

"In years he seemed but not impaired by years."

His health responded so faithfully to the inexorable loyalty of his character, as to go far towards justifying Buffon's theory, that the normal life of man is a hundred years, and that it is due not to the use but to the abuse of his organization, if he finds an earlier grave.

Meeting him some years ago and after a somewhat prolonged separation, I asked him particularly about his health. He said it was so perfect he hardly dared to speak of it. He was not conscious from one week to another, he said, of a physical sensation that he would have different; and was forgetting that he was liable to disease and decay. I asked him for his secret. He replied that he did not know that there was any secret about it, but he supposed he owed much of his health to a habit formed in early life, of devoting the first hour and a half or two hours after leaving his bed in the morning, to moderate gymnastic exercise, after which he took a bath and a light breakfast, consisting usually of milk with some kind of cereal food and fruit, but no meat. At dinner he ate pretty much what other people ate. His evening meal, when he did not dine late, was much the same as his breakfast. He drank sparingly of any thing stronger than water.

He avoided all condiments, he used neither tea nor coffee, and held tobacco in abhorrence. I remember the time when he could not stay in a room infected with the fumes of tobacco, though later in life he became less sensitive to its effects. He rarely allowed himself to be out of bed after ten at night, or in bed after five in the morning. To these habits and regimen he said he attributed in a great measure his exceptionally good health. Not many weeks before his death, and when recovering from a slight indisposition which he had been describing to me (he was then approaching his eighty-fourth year), I said: "I presume you have reduced your allowance of morning gymnastics?" "Not the width of your thumb-nail," was his prompt reply. "What," said I, "do you manage still 'to put in' your hour and a half every morning?" "Yes," he replied, "and sometimes more; frequently more."

Bryant had a marvellous memory. His familiarity with the English poets was such that when at sea, where he was always too ill to read much, he would beguile the time by reciting page after page from favorite poems. He assured me that, however long the voyage, he had never exhausted his resources. I once proposed to send for a copy of a magazine in which a new poem of his was announced to appear. "You need not send for it," said he: "I can give it to you." "Then you have a copy with you?" said I. "No," he replied, "but

I can recall it," and thereupon proceeded immediately to write it out. I congratulated him upon having such a faithful memory. "If allowed a little time," he replied, "I could recall every line of poetry I have ever written." Yet he rarely quoted, and never in a foreign tongue. This is the more noticeable, as he was scarcely less familiar with the languages and literatures of Germany, France, and Spain, of ancient and modern Greece, and of ancient and modern Rome, than with that of his own country, and he spoke all of those that are now classed among the living languages, except the modern Greek, with considerable facility and surprising correctness.

He rated his memory at its true value and never abused it. It was a blooded steed which he never degraded to the uses of a pack-horse. Hence he was fastidious about his reading as about his company, believing there was no worse thief than a bad book ; but he never tired of writers who have best stood the test of time. He had little taste for historical reading. Indeed, the habits of his mind were not at all in sympathy with the inductive method of reaching new truths or propagating them. He often deplored the increasing neglect of the old English classics, which our modern facilities for printing were displacing. Johnson's Lives of the Poets was one of his favorite books. Pope, who has educated more poets in the art of verse-making than any other modern author, was, from his early youth, his pocket companion. I think he had studied him more carefully than any other English writer, and was specially impressed by his wit.

One day as I was looking over the books on the shelves of his library at Roslyn, he called my attention to his position. "There," said he, "I have fallen quite accidentally into the precise attitude in which Pope is commonly represented, with his forehead resting on his fingers." He then got up to look for an illustration among his books. He did not find what he sought, but he brought two other editions, each representing Pope with an abundance of hair on his head, one an old folio containing a collection of Pope's verses written before he was twenty-five years of age.

I asked him if he had seen the new edition of Pope's works which Elwin was editing. He said he had not, nor heard of it. I then told him that Elwin left Pope scarcely a single estimable personal quality, and had stripped him of a good share of the literary laurels which he had hitherto worn in peace. He promptly said that he did not care to see it; that he was not disposed to trust such a judgment, however ingeniously defended. He then quoted Young's lines on Pope, "Sweet as his own Homer, his life melodious as his verse." "That," said he, "is the judgment of a contemporary." He then read some lines from other poets in farther defence of his favorite. He was unwilling to have his ideal of Pope disturbed, and when I suggested that he should get Elwin, he said : "No, I want no better edition than Warburton's, the edition that was in my father's library, and which I read when a boy." Bryant's admiration of Pope is the more remarkable, as two characters more unlike could not be readily imagined.

No prose writer since Queen Anne's period received from him such frequent commendation as Southey, whose prose seemed to have impressed him more than his poetry. He shared little of the popular enthusiasm for Macaulay. I don't remember to have heard him ever cite a line or an opinion of Byron, who was never one of his favorites. Some twenty-five or thirty years ago a person claiming to be a son of the poet appeared in New York with some poems and letters which he said had been written and given him by Byron, and for which he sought to find a market among our publishers. I spoke of the matter one day to Bryant, and his reply surpised me more than it would have done after my opinions of Byron were more settled. Looking up with an expression which implied more than he uttered, he said, "I think we have poems enough of Byron already."

Mr. Bryant used to say that a gentleman should never talk of his love-affairs or of his religion. So far as I know, he practiced as he preached. There was no subject which for many years appeared to occupy more of his thought than religion, none about which he seemed more willing to listen, but of his own spiritual experiences he was singularly reticent. I do not remember to have ever heard him define his creed upon any point of theology, or give utterance to a single dogma; neither do I believe such an utterance can be found in any of his writings; though so profound were his religious feelings and convictions, that they found expression in a series of exquisitely devotional hymns, which I trust may some day be given to the public. In matters of religion, his modesty was as conspicuous as in every thing else; he was never betrayed into citing his own example or his own opinions as an authority to any one else.

But it may be asked, had this "*monstrum perfectionis*" no faults? Bryant was born to the same sinful inheritance as the rest of us; but I can say of him with perfect truth, that with his faults he was always at war. No one better than he knew the enemies with which the human heart is always besieged,—the enemies of his own household; and few men ever fought them more valiantly, more persistently, or more successfully. Those who only knew him in his later years would scarcely believe that he had been endowed by nature with a very quick and passionate temper. He never entirely overcame it, but he held every impulse of his nature to such a rigorous accountability, that few have ever suspected the struggles with which he purchased the self-control which constituted one of the conspicuous graces of his character. Bryant had his faults, but he made of them agents of purification. He learned from them humility and faith, a wise distrust of himself, and an unfaltering trust in Him through whose aid he was strengthened to keep them in abeyance. By God's help he converted the tears of his angels into pearls.

It was this constant and successful warfare upon every unworthy and degrading propensity that sought an asylum in his heart, that made him such a moral force in the country, that invested any occasion to which he lent his presence with an especial dignity, that gave to his personal example a peculiar power and authority. No one could be much in the society of Bryant without feeling more respect for himself, without being conscious that his better nature had been awakened to a higher activity, without an increased reluctance to say or do any thing which Bryant himself under similar circumstances would probably not have said or done.

# CHAPTER VIII.

## LONGFELLOW AND WHITTIER.

William Winter's Reminiscences of Longfellow—A conversation concerning "Evangeline" and other poems—Pen pictures of Whittier.

Of the many sketches of Longfellow which have appeared since his death, there are none which give a juster and more appreciative view of the poet as he appeared in his daily habits than the reminiscences contributed by Mr. William Winter to the New York *Tribune*, from which I quote the following paragraphs:

WILLIAM WINTER'S REMINISCENCES OF
LONGFELLOW.

My remembrance of Longfellow goes back to a period about thirty years ago, when he was a professor in Harvard University. I had read every line he had then published, and such was the affection he inspired, even in a boyish mind, that on many a summer night I walked several miles to his house, only to put my hands on the latch of his gate which he himself had touched. More than any one else among the many famous persons whom, since then, it has been my fortune to know, he aroused this feeling of mingled tenderness and reverence. I saw him often—walking in the streets of Cambridge, or looking over the books, in the old shop of Ticknor & Fields, at the corner of Washington and School streets in Boston—long before I was honored with his personal acquaintance; and I observed him closely, as a youth naturally does the object of his honest admiration. His natural dignity and grace, and the beautiful refinement of his countenance, together with his perfect taste in dress, and the exquisite simplicity of his manners, made him the absolute ideal of what a poet should be. His voice, too, was soft, sweet, and musical; and, like his face, it had the innate charm of tranquillity. His eyes were bluish-gray, very bright and brave, changeable under the influence of emotion (as, afterward, I saw), but mostly calm, grave, attentive, and gentle. The habitual expression of his face was not that of sadness; and yet it was sad. Perhaps it may best be described as that of serious and tender thoughtfulness. He had conquered his own sorrows thus far, but the sorrows of others threw their shadow over him, as he sweetly and humanely says in his pathetic ballad of "The Bridge."

It was in April, 1854, that I became personally acquainted with Longfellow, and he was the first

literary friend I ever had—greeting me as a young
aspirant in literature, and holding out to me the
hand of fellowship and encouragement. He allowed
me to dedicate to him a volume of my verses, published in that year, being the first of my ventures.
They were such bad verses that I hope I shall
never see them again; yet he was tolerant of them,
becuuse he knew the sincerity of heart and ambition of spirit that lay beneath them, and in his
far-reaching charity and prescience he must have
thought that something good might come, even of
such a poor beginning. At all events, where others
were cold, or satirical, or contemptuous, he was
kind and cordial and full of cheer. A few words in
commendation of some of these verses had been
written by N. P. Willis, and the paragraph happened
to come in his way. He was sincerely pleased with
it, and I can hear now the gentle, hearty tone in
which he spoke of it, turning to Mrs. Longfellow,
who was present, and saying, with an obvious relish
of good-will: "There is a great deal of kindness in
Willis' nature." This was a little trait, but it is of
little traits that the greatest human character is
composed. Goodness, generosity, and a large libe-
rality of judgment were, in his character, conspicuous elements. His spontaneous desire—the natural
instinct of his great heart and massive philosophic
mind—was to be helpful; to lift up the lowly; to
strengthen the weak; to bring out the best in every

person; to dry every tear and make every pathway smooth. It is saying but little to say that he never said a harsh word, except against injustice and wrong. He was the natural friend and earnest advocate of every good cause and right idea. His words about the absent were always considerate and gentle, and he never lost a practical opportunity of doing good.

For the infirmities of humanity he was charity itself, and he shrank from harshness as from a positive sin. "It is the prerogative of the poet," he once said to me in those old days, "to give pleasure; but it's the critic's province to give pain." He had, indeed, but a slender esteem for the critic's province. Yet his tolerant nature found excuses for even as virulent and hostile a critic as his assailant and traducer, Edgar Allan Poe, of whom I have heard him speak with genuine pity. His words were few and unobtrusive, and they clearly indicated his consciousness that Poe had grossly abused and maligned him; but instead of resentment for injury, they displayed only sorrow for an unfortunate and half-crazed adversary. There was a little volume of Poe's poems—an English edition—on the library table, and at sight of this I was prompted to ask Longfellow if Poe had ever personally met him, "because," I said, "if he had known you, it is impossible he could have written about you in such a manner." He

CRAIGIE HOUSE.

answered that he had never seen Poe, and that the bitterness was doubtless due to a deplorable literary jealousy. Then, after a pause of musing, he added very gravely : " My works seemed to give him much trouble first and last; but Mr. Poe is dead and buried, and I am alive and still writing—and that is the end of the matter. I never condescended to answer Mr. Poe's attacks ; and I would advise you now, at the outset of your literary career, never to take notice of any attacks that may be made upon you. Let them all pass." He then took up the volume of Poe, and turning the leaves, particularly commended the stanzas entitled "For Annie" and "The Haunted Palace." Then, still speaking of criticism, he mentioned the great number of newspaper and magazine articles, about his own writings, that were received by him—sent, apparently, by their writers. "I look at the first few lines," he said, "and if I find that the article has been written in a pleasant spirit, I read it through ; but if I find that the intention is to wound, I drop the paper into my fire, and so dismiss it. In that way one escapes much annoyance."

Longfellow liked to talk of young poets, and he had an equally humorous and kind way of noticing the foibles of the literary character. Standing in the porch one summer day, and observing the noble elms in front of his house, he recalled a visit made to him, long before, by one of the many bards, now extinct, who are embalmed in Griswold. Then suddenly assuming a burly, martial air, he seemed to reproduce for me the exact figure and manner of the youthful enthusiast—who had tossed back his long hair, gazed approvingly on the elms, and in a deep voice exclaimed, "I see, Mr. Longfellow, that you have many trees—I love trees!" "It was," said the poet, "as if he gave a certificate to all the neighboring vegetation." A few words like these, said in Longfellow's peculiar, dry, humorous manner, with just a twinkle of the eye and a quietly droll inflection of the voice, had a certain charm of mirth that cannot be described. It was that same demure playfulness which led him, when writing, to speak of the lady who wore flowers "on the congregation side of her bonnet," or to extol those broad, magnificent Western roads, which "dwindle to a squirrel-track, and run up a tree." He had no particle of the acidity of sparkling and biting wit; but he had abundant playful humor, that was full of kindness, and that toyed good-naturedly with all the trifles of life. That such a sense of fun should be amused by the ludicrous peculiarities of a juvenile bard was inevitable. He had himself passed through the grotesque and singular period.

I recall many talks with him, about poetry and the avenues of literary labor, and the discipline of the mind in youth. His counsel was always summed up in two words—calmness and patience. He did

HENRY W. LONGFELLOW.

not believe in seeking experience or in going to meet burdens. "What you desire will come, if you will but wait for it"—that he said to me again and again. "My great ambition once was," he remarked, "to edit a magazine. Since then the opportunity has been offered to me many times, and I did not take it and would not." That same night he spoke of his first poem—the first that ever was printed—and described his trepidation, when going, in the evening, to drop the precious manuscript into the editor's box. This was at a weekly newspaper office in Portland, Maine, when he was a boy. Publication day arrived, and the paper came out—but not a word of the poem. "But I had another copy," he said, "and I immediately sent it to the rival weekly, and the next week it was published." And then he described his exultation and inexpressible joy and pride, when, having bought a copy of the paper, still damp from the press, and walked with it into a by-street of the town, he saw, for the first time, a poem of his own actually in print. "I have never since had such a thrill of delight," he said, "over any of my publications."

His sense of humor found especial pleasure in the inappropriate words that were sometimes said to him by persons whose design it was to be complimentary, and he would relate, with a keen relish of their pleasantry, anecdotes, against himself, to illustrate this form of social blunder. Years ago he told me, at Cambridge, about the strange gentleman who was led up to him and introduced at Newport, and who straightway said with enthusiastic fervor: "Mr. Longfellow, I have long desired the honor of knowing you! Sir, I am one of *the few* men who have read your 'Evangeline.'" This anecdote, in recent days, he coupled with another, about an English lady who, on being introduced, exclaimed: "Why, Mr. Longfellow, I thought you were dead!" "No, madam, you see I take the liberty of living." "Yes; but I thought at least you belonged to Washington's time." Another of his favorites was related to me a day or two after it occurred. The poet's rule was to reserve the morning for work, and visitors were not received before twelve o'clock, noon. One morning a man forced his way past the servant who had opened the hall-door, and burst in upon the presence of the astonished author in his library; and thereupon ensued this remarkable conversation: "Mr. Longfellow, you 're a poet, I believe." "Well, sir, some persons have said so." "All right, Mr. Longfellow! Poet it is! Now, I 've called here to see if I could n't git you to write some poetry for me to have printed and stuck onto my medicine bottles. You see, I go round sellin' this medicine, and if you 'll do it, it 'll help immensely; and I 'll just tell you right now, if you give me the poetry, I 'll give you a bottle of the carminative—and it's $1 a bottle." For the full enjoyment of this story it was needful to see the poet's face, and hear the delicious, bland tone of voice in which he added: "The idea of its being a carminative, of all things." More than twenty-four years ago he told me that incident, sitting by the wide fireplace, in the library back of his study. As I write his words now, the wind seems again to be moaning in the chimney, and the fire-light flickers upon his pale, handsome, happy face, and already silvered hair. He took such delight in any bit of quiet fun like that! He was so gracious, so kind, so wishful to make every one happy that came near him! And now he is gone forever!

A correspondent of the *Philadelphia Press*, writing in the early part of 1881, gives the substance of an interesting conversation held with the poet in regard to his own works, in the following account of

### A VISIT TO LONGFELLOW.

I had hardly time to run my eye over the walls clad with the rich mementoes of early times and full of the memories of great events, both in war and peace, and admire the simple comforts of the old parlor, furnished as in primitive times where culture and means resided, before an old gentleman stepped briskly across the hall from the room directly opposite, and, extending his hand, heartily welcomed me to his interesting home. It was the author of "Evangeline." I was disappointed in his appearance, for I had fancied from his portraits a large, brawny man, something like Walt Whitman, barring the tendency of that eccentric genius to *abandon* in dress. Instead, here was a man of medium size, a lithe, finely moulded, rather than sturdy form,—"a man of genteel mould," as it were. The light in his eye and the warmth of his hand showed that the eighty years which have rolled over his head have not lain heavily upon him. His face is full of genial expression, and the kindly eyes give it a charm which cannot be pictured with words.

"Step into my library," said he, after the greeting, and he showed the way across the hall. At first the conversation took a wide range. The poet was inclined to ask questions about men and current events, and it was quite a time before the drift of chat turned upon what he was doing, had done, and expected to accomplish. "I am not doing much these days," he said; "simply keeping from getting rusty," and he cast his eye around the room at the many evidences of work lying about, as much as to say, "You can see for yourself how much that is." Then the talk turned upon his poems and his already published works, and I ventured to express a curiosity to know the history of his poem, "The Hymn of the Moravian Nuns."

"It was one of my early works; I wrote it while at college," he replied. "I read in a newspaper a story that the Moravian women at Bethlehem had embroidered a banner and presented it to Pulaski. The story made an impression upon my mind, and one idle day I wrote the poem. I called them Moravian nuns, because I had gathered from something I had heard or read that they were called nuns. I suppose I should have said Moravian sisters, but the change does n't spoil the romance. I often felt a curiosity to go and see the people whose patriotic action furnished the theme for this poem, and whose peculiar customs and steady thrift have gained them the admiration of the world."

Expressing a preference for his "Evangeline," I ventured to say, "I see you located the final scene of that beautiful story in Philadelphia." "Yes, sir. The poem is one of my favorites also—as much, perhaps, on account of the manner in which I got the groundwork for it as anything else." "What is the story, please?" "I will tell you. Hawthorne came to dine with me one day, and brought a friend with him from Salem. While at the dinner Mr Hawthorne's friend said to me, 'I have been trying to get Hawthorne to write a story about the banishment of the Acadians from Acadia, founded upon the life of a young Acadian girl who was then separated from her lover, spent the balance of her life searching for him, and when both were old found him dying in a hospital.' 'Yes,' said Hawthorne, 'but there is nothing in that for a story.' I caught the thought at once that it would make a striking picture if put in verse, and said, 'Hawthorne, give it to me for a poem, and promise me that you will not write about it until I have written the poem.'

"Hawthorne readily assented to my request, and it was agreed that I should use his friend's story for verse whenever I had the time and inclination to write it. In 1825 I started for Europe, and when in New York concluded I would visit Philadelphia, and so went over. It was in the spring about this time, and the country was as beautiful as it is to-day. I spent a week in the Quaker City, stopping at the old Mansion House, on Third Street, near Walnut. It was one of the best hotels I ever stopped at, and at that time perhaps the best in the country. It had been the private residence of the wealthy Binghams, and was kept by a man named Head. The table was excellent, and the bedchambers were splendidly furnished, and were great, large, airy rooms, as large as this,"—turning around and surveying the ample library room in which we were seated. "It has given way now to the demands of business, I believe, for when I was last there I could hardly recognize the place where it stood. During this visit I spent much time looking about, and Philadelphia is one of the places which made a lasting impression upon me and left its mark upon my later work. Even the streets of Philadelphia make rhyme.

> "Chestnut, Walnut, Spruce, and Pine,
> Market, Arch, Race, and Vine."

"I got the climax of 'Evangeline' from Philadelphia, you know, and it was singular how I happened to do so. I was passing down Spruce street one day toward my hotel after a walk, when my attention was attracted to a large building, with beautiful trees about it, inside of a high enclosure. I walked along until I came to the great gate, and then stepped inside and looked carefully over the place. The charming picture of lawn, flower-beds, and shade which it presented made an impression which has never left me, and twenty-four years after, when I came to write 'Evangeline,' I located the final scene, the meeting between Evangeline and Gabriel, and the death at this poorhouse, and the burial in an old Catholic graveyard not far away, which I found by chance in another of my walks. It is purely a fancy sketch, and the name of Evangeline was coined to complete the story. The incident Mr. Hawthorne's friend gave me, and my visit to the poorhouse in Philadelphia, gave me the groundwork of the poem."

"The claim is that the Quaker almshouse on Walnut Street, near Third, is the one referred to in 'Evangeline.'"

"No, that is not so. I remember that place distinctly. It is the old poorhouse I referred to, which stood on the square between Spruce and Pine and Tenth and Eleventh streets."

Mr. Longfellow then took from an adjoining room a picture of the old Quaker almshouse, and explained that the spot which attracted his attention and marked Philadelphia for the final act of "Evangeline" was not this old institution, as had been so often claimed.

"Have you ever been in Philadelphia since the visit more than half a century ago?"

"Yes, twice. In 1833, and again during the Centennial. The scene of one of my latest poems is located near Philadelphia. 'Old St. David's at Radnor'—I refer to. I got the impressions for this poem during the centennial year, when I was there attending the exhibition. I was stopping at Rosemont, and one day drove over to Radnor. Old St. David's Church, with its charming and picturesque surroundings, attracted my attention. Its diminutive size, peculiar architecture, the little rectory in the grove, the quiet churchyard where mad Anthony Wayne is buried, the great tree which stands at the gateway, and the pile of gray stone which makes the old church, and is almost hidden by the climbing ivy,—all combine to make it a gem for a fancy picture."

## JOHN G. WHITTIER.

Mr. Whittier's life has been a quiet and secluded one. Not caring to obtrude his personality upon the public, he has especially shunned the Boswells of the press, and there are extant few personal sketches of him. Here, however, is a little vignette taken by Miss Bremer when the poet was about forty years of age:

He has a good exterior, a figure slender and tall, a beautiful head with refined features, black eyes full of fire, dark complexion, a fine smile, and lively but very nervous manner. Both soul and spirit have overstrained the nervous cords and wasted the body. He belongs to those natures who would advance with firmness and joy to martyrdom in a good cause, and yet who are never comfortable in society, and who look as if they would run out of the door every moment. He lives with his mother and sister in a country-house to which I have promised to go. I feel that I should enjoy myself with Whittier, and could make him feel at ease with me. I know from my own experience what this nervous bashfulness, caused by the over-exertion of the brain, requires, and how persons who suffer therefrom ought to be met and treated.

An essayist who met Whittier later in life,

in 1864, tells us that his first thought on seeing him was, "the head of a Hebrew prophet!" "Indeed, the impression was so strong as to induce some little feeling of embarrassment. It seemed slightly awkward and insipid to be meeting a prophet here in a parlor and in a spruce masquerade of modern costume, shaking hands, and saying, 'Happy to meet you,' after the fashion of our feeble civilities."

## CHAPTER IX.

### LOWELL AND HOLMES.

*Description of the Lowell household by Miss Bremer—Lowell's appearance and conversation by Justin McCarthy—Oliver Wendell Holmes as a lecturer.*

OF Mr. Lowell, in his early manhood, Miss Bremer, the Swedish novelist, has given the following as her impressions in the "Homes of the New World."

I have now been a week at Cambridge with the Lowells; they will have me stay, and I am quite willing to stay, because I am well off to my heart's content in this excellent and agreeable home. The house and a small quantity of land which surrounds it belong to the father of the poet, Dr. Lowell, a handsome old man, universally beloved and respected, and the oldest minister in Massachusetts. The whole family assembles every day for morning and evening prayers around the venerable old man, and he it is who blesses every meal. With him live his youngest son, the poet, and his wife; such a handsome and happy young couple as one can hardly imagine. He is full of life and youthful ardor; she, as gentle, as delicate, and as fair as a lily, and one of the most lovable women that I have seen in this country, because her beauty is full of soul and grace, as is every thing which she does or says. The young couple belong to the class of those of whom one can be quite sure; one could not for an hour, nay, not for half an hour, be doubtful of them. She, like him, has a poetical tendency, and has also written, anonymously, some poems, remarkable for their deep and tender feeling, especially maternal, but her mind has more philosophical depth than his. Singularly enough, I did not discern in him that deeply earnest spirit which charmed me in many of his poems. He seems to me occasionally to be brilliant, witty, gay, especially in the evening, when he has what he calls his "evening fever," and his talk is then like an incessant play of fireworks. I find him very agreeable and amiable; he seems to have many friends, mostly young men. As one of his merits, I reckon his being so fascinated by his little wife, because I am so myself. There is a trace of beauty and taste in everything she touches, whether of mind or body; and above all, she beautifies life. Among other beautiful things which she has created around her in her home, I have remarked a little basin full of beautiful stones and shells, which she herself collected; they lie glittering in water clear as crystal, and round them is a border of coral.

As a counterpart to the above may be added Justin McCarthy's portrait of the poet in his maturer years.

##### McCARTHY'S SKETCH OF JAMES RUSSELL LOWELL.

There is something very English-looking in Lowell; he has nothing of what we in this country regard as the American type about him. His strong square form, his massive head, with the bright cheery expression, and the quiet good-humored eyes, are almost exactly what people think a genuine Briton ought to have. His appearance naturally surprises, at first, those who had known him beforehand only through his books. There is so much delicacy and subtleness in his graver poems and his essays, his criticisms and his thoughts are alike so finely traced out, that we are not prepared for so robust and vigorous a type of man. We had formed in our minds the idea, perhaps, of a pale and deep-eyed scholar, and we see a broad-shouldered, full-bearded, strong, and cheery Anglo-Saxon. Yet, after a while, the idea begins somehow to restore and reassert itself. There is a certain suggestion of easy and meditative indecision about the eyes and mouth of the strongly built scholar which helps us to recognize the author of the over-thoughtful poems and the exquisitely poetic essays. In the course of a rather protracted trial, about which people in this country were in the habit of talking a little lately, a lady, called as a witness to identity, observed that she did not at first exactly recognize the rightful heir in the stout personage who stood before her, but that she seemed to see the rightful heir somehow hovering about him. One who first sees Lowell is perhaps in a somewhat similar condition; there before you is the author of the "Biglow Papers" plainly enough—stout, strong, and ready to fight against any manner of sham,—but where is the poet of "The Cathedral," and "Under the Willows"?—where is the author of the refined and poetic essays? But when he speaks, and the light of varying expression passes over his face, one begins to see the poet and the scholar hovering about Hosea Biglow somehow. One soon learns to understand how it was that Hosea Biglow had so much fancy and poetry in his fibrous nature, and how the enthusiast of the "Commemoration Ode" could sometimes stop to think, amid the fervor of all his patriotic emotion.

It would be superfluous to say that Lowell has for more than twenty years been—perhaps not always to his own satisfaction—one of the celebrities of Boston and its neighborhood. Truly Boston is a place in which a reputation is worth having. The community is not too large to know its celebrities. A good thing said by a man echoes all round his

sphere of existence; the men of letters all know each
other, and are friends; the whole school of poets,
philosophers, and humorists dine together frequently
at one table; the "Saturday Club" gathers them all
at its pleasant board. Boston seems to me to be a
good deal like what Edinburgh must have been in
its best days of literature. In London, and even to
some extent in New York, people have to live in
cliques and *coteries*. This is so even where they
belong to the same profession and would be friendly
if they could. There are only local acquaintance-
ships and fellowships in a metropolis like ours. No
fervor of friendship could conquer our distances;
it is morally impossible that Kensington and Belsize
Park could have frequent and familiar intercourse.
But Boston is of delightful smallness; even if we
take in Cambridge, it is still of charmingly convenient dimensions. Literary men can really know
each other there, and have sympathies and friend-
ships. There is something peculiarly friendly about
the very aspect of the place. Its literary people,
and indeed its people generally, are said to be rather
conceited on the subject of their city and its dignity.
The journals of other cities are never weary of making jokes about the Bostonian's faith in the theory
that the world takes its time from Boston. It is commonly averred throughout many States of the Union
that a Massachusetts man regards the frog-pond on
Boston Common as the noblest expanse of water in

existence. "And now, Mr. ——," said a chief of Boston letters to an author from New York, who had just made a great literary success, "now, when are you coming to live in Boston?"

In conversation with Mr. Lowell, people are some times surprised to find that there is not more of the Radical in his political views. He never could have been a fanatic, but I cannot help thinking that a certain conservative tendency, so hard to keep off from advancing years, is already and prematurely showing itself in Mr. Lowell's views of life. His country has had to pass through so many terrible ordeals in his time, that perhaps he is more anxious that for a while she should rest and be thankful than do any thing else. A man with such a mind and temperament as his could have but little sympathy with some of the rather aggressive and enterprising forms in which new ideas have lately manifested themselves now and then in the United States. I have no doubt that he thought the process of pouring the new wine into the old bottles had been carried on with rather too liberal and reckless a hand in the sudden elevation of the negro population to full citizenship everywhere over the States; and he must have found some of the Woman's Rights "developments" rather trying occasionally. Perhaps he thinks America has had lately more sentiment of all kinds than was quite good for her. Certainly his conversation on political and social subjects seems of a much shrewder and less enthusiastic kind than one might have expected who remembered the early apostrophes to Lamartine and Kossuth, and the fervor, hardly veiled even in sarcasm, of the "Biglow Papers." Without suggesting any comparison between two men and two careers so unlike, I cannot help thinking that Mr. Lowell holds now, with regard to the politics of the United States, something like the views which Mr. Bright is understood to entertain with regard to those of England. Each is content with a great good done, but sees that it cost trouble and sacrifice to do it, and is not anxious that any new enterprises should soon be undertaken. People who have lately conversed with Mr. Bright, and had only known him before through newspapers, are always telling us how surprised they were to find him so conservative in his opinions. I can easily understand that the same thing might be said of Mr. Lowell.

But whatever this person or that may think of the particular views he happens to express, I, for myself, very much doubt whether Mr. Lowell is ever more brilliant and delightful than he shows himself in conversation. He is not, by any means, what people would have called some years ago a great talker; he never keeps all the talk to himself, or pours forth long and flowing sentences, or showers down the sparkling spray of witticisms over an admiring and watchful company. He is not in the least like a Coleridge or a Macaulay ; nor does he rush along in unbroken monologues like his countryman, the late Mr. Seward ; nor has he the overpowering conversational energy of another countryman of his, the late Mr. Charles Sumner. The charm of Mr. Lowell's conversation is, that it is conversation, and not soliloquy, or sermon, or the elaborate display of the professional wit. Mr. Lowell talks, in fact, after the fashion of ordinary people, except that he always talks well ; that when most others of us say commonplace things, he says something brilliant, or deep, or thoughtful, or sometimes poetic, or not uncommonly paradoxical. He suggests, perhaps, some new and odd way of looking at an old subject ; he extracts some humorous conceit from a very familiar thought or fact ; he draws at will upon the rich resources of a scholarship the most varied and liberal. Few Englishmen are so well acquainted, I should think, with English literature at its best periods, and he appears to have a not less thorough acquaintance with the literature of Greece and Rome, of France and Germany, of Italy and Spain. Nothing is more perilous than any effort to reproduce in cold blood some bright thoughts suggested in passing conversation ; and I almost fear to do Mr. Lowell an injustice by attempting to describe the impression produced on me by this or that phrase or suggestion of his. Two or three points, however, I feel tempted to recall.

He talked once of collisions at sea, suggested by some recent casualty, and he mentioned how much he had been struck by a passage he had read in the evidence of a man saved from such a calamity. The man stated that the vessel in which he sailed ran right into another vessel, literally cutting her in two ; and all he could tell of the passengers in the destroyed ship was, that he became conscious of seeing a person who was lying in his berth reading a newspaper by the light of a lamp, and this person looked up startled for a moment, and no more was seen of ship or passengers. Mr. Lowell made, in a few words, and without any appearance of either painting or moralizing, a wonderful picture of this little incident, of the quiet reader suddenly startled from his paper, and meeting in the gleam of light the pale, horrified face of his innocent destroyer, and then gone forever into the darkness. Another time he told us of some wine of marvellous price, of which he had drunk one glass, for the sake, as he put it, of swallowing so much liquid wealth ; and the number of quaint conceits which he caused to come up like bubbles on the surface of that precious glass, the variety of ways in which he illustrated the possible value of the draught, might have either delighted an Epicurean or a teetotaller according as one chose to look at it, or according as he supposed Mr. Lowell to be in jest or earnest. His love of paradoxes made a visitor from England once say that he felt reminded, while listening to him, of some of Mr. Lowe's more remarkable speeches. Oddly enough, Mr. Lowell mentioned the fact that he once crossed the Atlantic with Mr. Lowe, and found the conversation of the latter peculiarly interesting and congenial. Speaking of English poets, Mr. Lowell observed of one of them, that he "started with a finer outfit" than any other, but that his stock got so crowded up, he became less able to use it to any purpose the longer he went on. Of a certain tendency in the modern poetry of England, he quietly observed, "I don't believe true art ever goes about patting the passions on the back."

Mr. Lowell, it will probably occur to the reader, is more of a literary man than most of our living English poets, and more of a poet than most of our literary men. He is more fully rounded, one might say, than most of his English peers and rivals.

Of Oliver Wendell Holmes, the genial autocrat, poet, and professor, Mr. David Macrae, a travelling Scotchman who published a book about America in 1864, presents the following sketch, taken in the lecture-hall of the medical department of Harvard College.

### DR. HOLMES AS A LECTURER.

I was glad to hear that the opening of the medical classes would give me an opportunity of hearing Oliver Wendell Holmes deliver the inaugural lecture. Mr. Fields, the publisher, who went with me, took me round to the museum behind the lecture-hall, where we found a number of the literary and scientific men of Boston assembled to accompany Dr. Holmes to the platform. The doctor himself was there, but was altogether a different-looking man from what I had supposed him to be. I had conceived of him, for what reason I know not, possibly from his poetry, as a tall, thin, dark-eyed, brilliant-looking man. This is not, perhaps, the conception one gets from his "Autocrat of the Breakfast-Table"; but I read his poems first, and first impressions are apt to remain. Holmes is a plain little dapper man, his short hair brushed down like a boy's, but turning gray now; a trifle of furzy hair under his ears; a powerful jaw, and a thick, strong underlip that gives decision to his look, with a dash of pertness. In conversation, he is animated and cordial,—sharp, too, taking the word out of one's mouth. When Mr. Fields said, "I sent the boy this——" "Yes; I got them," said Holmes. He told me I should hear some references to Dr. John Brown of Edinburgh in his lecture; also some thoughts he had taken from Dr. Brown's fine essay on Locke and Sydenham. "But you see," he added with a smile, "I always tell when I steal any thing!"

Near us, under one of the lofty windows, two men were standing, whom I would have travelled many a league to meet. One of them was Professor Louis Agassiz—big, massive, genial-looking; the rich healthy color on his broad face still telling of the Old World from which he came,—altogether a man who, but for his dark, keen eyes, would look more like a jovial English squire than a devotee of science. Beside him stood a man of strangely different build—a gaunt, long-limbed man,—dressed in a high-collared surtout, his piquant New England face peering down over the old-fashioned black kerchief that swathed his long, thin neck. It was Emerson, the glorious transcendentalist of Concord. He stood in an easy, contemplative attitude, with his hands loosely folded in front, and his head slightly inclined. He has the queerest New England face, with thin features, prominent hatchet nose, and a smile of childlike sweetness and simplicity arching the face and drawing deep curves down the cheek. Eyes, too, full of sparkling geniality, and yet in a moment turning cold, clear, and searching, like the eyes of a god. I remember, when introduced to him, how kindly he took my hand, and with that smile still upon his face, peered deep with those calm blue eyes into mine.

When the hour arrived we went into the lecture room. Let me try to bring up the scene again. The room is crowded to the door,—so crowded that many of the students have to sit on the steps leading up between the sections of concentric seats, and stand crushed three or four deep in the passages along the walls. What a sea of pale faces, and dark, thoughtful eyes !

Holmes, Emerson, and Agassiz are cheered loudly as they enter and take their seats. The Principal opens proceedings with a short prayer, the audience remaining seated. Dr. Holmes now gets up, steps forward to the high desk amidst loud cheers, puts his eye-glasses across his nose, arranges his manuscript, and, without any prelude, begins. The little man, in his dress coat, stands very straight, a little stiff about the neck, as if he feels that he cannot afford to lose any thing of his stature. He reads with a sharp, percussive articulation, is very deliberate and formal at first, but becomes more animated as he goes on. He would even gesticulate if the desk were not so high, for you see the arm that lies on the desk beside his manuscript giving a nervous quiver at emphatic points. The subject of this lecture is the spirit in which medical students should go into their work,—now as students, afterward as practitioners. He warns them against looking on it as a mere lucrative employment. "Don't be like the man who said, 'I suppose I *must* go and earn that d——d guinea!'" He enlivens his lecture with numerous jokes and brilliant sallies of wit, and at every point hitches up his head, looks through his glasses at his audience as he finishes his sentence, and then shuts his mouth pertly with his underlip as if he said, "There, laugh at that!"

Emerson sits listening, with his arms folded loosely on his breast,—that queer smile of his effervescing at every joke into a silent laugh, that runs up into his eyes and quivers at the corners of his eyebrows, like sunlight in the woods. Beside him sits Agassiz, leaning easily back in his chair, trifling with the thick watch-guard that glitters on his capacious white waistcoat, and looking like a man who has just had dinner and is disposed to take a pleasant view of things.

Holmes is becoming more animated. His arm is in motion now, indulging in mild movements toward the desk, as if he meant to kill a fly, but always repents and does n't. He shows less mercy on the persons and opinions that he has occasion to criticise. He comes down sharply on "the quacks, with or without diplomas, who think that the chief end of man is to support the apothecary." He has a passing hit at Carlyle's "Shooting Niagara," and his discovery of the legitimate successor of Jesus Christ in the drill-sergeant. He has also a fling at Dr. Cumming of London, and "his prediction that the world is to come to an end next year or next week, weather permitting, but very sure that the weather will be unpropitious."

The lecture lasted about an hour, and at its close was applauded again and again, Holmes being a great favorite with the students. I met him afterward at a dinner given to Longfellow and his literary friends, in congratulation on the completion of the poet's translation of Dante ; and hoped there to enjoy one of the autocrat's after-dinner speeches, which are said to be among his most brilliant performances. Longfellow, however, unlike most Americans, shrinks from any kind of public speaking himself, and Mr. Fields came round at dessert to inform us that Longfellow had declared that if he had to make a speech he should be in torment all the evening and lose the enjoyment of his dinner. It had, therefore, been resolved that there should be no speeches; so Holmes' power as an *improvisatore* had no opportunity for exercising itself that night.

## CHAPTER X.

### NATHANIEL HAWTHORNE.

*His cheerfulness—Some reminiscences by James T. Fields, George William Curtis, and others—His shyness and love of seclusion—His personal appearance.*

IN her preface to the English "Note-Books," the wife of Hawthorne protests against "the often-expressed opinion that Mr. Hawthorne was gloomy and morbid." "He had," she says, "the inevitable pensiveness and gravity of a person who possessed what a friend of his called 'the awful power of insight'; but his mood was always cheerful and equal, and his mind peculiarly healthful, and the airy splendor of his wit and humor was the life of his home. He saw too far to be despondent, though his vivid sympathies and shaping imagination often made him sad in behalf of others. He also perceived morbidness, wherever it existed, instantly, as if by the illu-

mination of his steady cheer, and he had the plastic power of putting himself into each person's situation and of looking from every point of view, which made his charity most comprehensive. From this cause he necessarily attracted confidences and became confessor to very many sinning and suffering souls, to whom he gave tender sympathy and help, while resigning judgment to the Omniscient and All-Wise."

Mr. James T. Fields tells us that he has often been asked if all Hawthorne's moods were sombre, and if he was never jolly sometimes like other people, to which he answers:

Indeed he was, and although the humorous side of Hawthorne was not easily or often discoverable, yet have I seen him marvellously moved to fun, and no man laughed more heartily in his way over a good story. Wise and witty, H., in whom wisdom and wit are so ingrained that age only increases his subtle spirit and greatly enhances the power of his cheerful temperament, always had the talismanic faculty of breaking up that thoughtfully sad face into mirthful waves; and I remember how Hawthorne writhed with hilarious delight over Prof. L——'s account of a butcher who remarked that "Idees had got afloat in the public mind with respect to sassingers." I once told him of a young woman who brought in a manuscript and said, as she placed it in my hands, "I don't know what to do with myself sometimes, I'm so filled with *mammoth thoughts.*" A series of convulsive efforts to suppress explosive laughter followed, which I remember to this day.

And here is Mr. Fields' description of a sea voyage (the return trip to America), on which Hawthorne's powers of badinage were exerted to keep up the spirits of his travelling companions.

Hawthorne's love for the sea amounted to a passionate worship; and while I (the worst sailor probably on this planet) was longing, spite of the good company on board, to reach land as soon as possible, Hawthorne was constantly saying in his quiet, earnest way, "I should like to sail on and on forever and never touch the shore again." He liked to stand alone in the bows of the ship and see the sun go down, and he was never tired of walking the deck at midnight. I used to watch his dark solitary figure, pacing up and down some unfrequented part of the vessel, musing and half melancholy. Sometimes he would lie down beside me and commiserate my unquiet condition. Sea-sickness, he declared, he could not understand, and was constantly

recommending most extraordinary dishes and drinks
"all made out of the *artist's* brain," which he said
were sovereign remedies for nautical sickness. I
remember to this day some of the preparations
which, in his revelry of fancy, he would advise me
to take, a farrago of good things almost rivalling
"Oberon's Feast" spread out so daintily in Her-
rick's "Hesperides." He thought, at first, if I
could bear a few roc's eggs beaten up by a mer-
maid on a dolphin's back, I might be benefited.
He decided that a gruel made from a sheaf of Rob-
in Hood's arrows would be strengthening. When
suffering pain, "a right gude willie-waught," or a
stiff cup of hemlock of the Socrates brand, before
retiring, he considered very good. He said he had
heard recommended a dose of salts distilled from
the tears of Niobe, but he did n't approve of that
remedy. He observed that he had a high opinion
of hearty food, such as potted owl with Minerva
sauce, airy tongues of sirens, stewed ibis, livers of
Roman Capitol geese, the wings of a phœnix not too
much done, love-lorn nightingales cooked briskly
over Aladdin's lamp, chicken pies made of fowls
raised by Mrs. Carey, nautilus chowder, and the
like. Examining my garments one day as I lay on
deck, he thought I was not warmly enough clad,
and he recommended, before I took another voyage, that I should fit myself out in Liverpool with a
good warm shirt from the shop of Nessus & Co., in

Bond Street, where I could also find stout seven-league boots to keep out the damp. He knew another shop, he said, where I could buy raven-down stockings, and sable clouds with a silver lining, most warm and comfortable for a sea-voyage.

His own appetite was excellent, and day after day he used to come on deck after dinner and describe to me what he had eaten. Of course his accounts were always exaggerations, for my amusement. I remember one night he gave me a running catalogue of what food he had partaken during the day, and the sum total was convulsing from its absurdity. Among the viands he had consumed, I remember he stated there were "several yards of steak" and a "whole warrenful of Welsh rabbits." The "divine spirit of humor" was upon him during many of these days at sea, and he revelled in it like a careless child.

In general company, Hawthorne was silent and reserved. He was intensely shy, so much so that he has been known to leave the high way for the fields rather than encounter a group of approaching villagers. He loved to go on solitary walks, he sought out secluded places where he could muse and dream without fear of disturbance. Once he brought Mr. Fields to one of these haunts, and bade him lie down on the grass, and watch the clouds float above, and hear the birds sing. "As we steeped ourselves in the delicious idleness, he began to murmur some half-forgotten lines from Thomson's 'Seasons,' which he said had been favorites of his from boyhood. While we lay there, hidden in the grass, we heard approaching footsteps, and Hawthorne hurriedly whispered, 'Duck! or we shall be interrupted by somebody.' The solemnity of his manner, and the thought of the down-flat position in which we had both placed ourselves to avoid being seen, threw me into a foolish, semi-hysterical fit of laughter, and when he nudged me, and again whispered more lugubriously than ever, 'Heaven help me, Mr. —— is close upon us!' I felt convinced that if the thing went further, suffocation, in my case at least, must ensue."

Mr. George William Curtis gives these reminiscences of the author of the "Scarlet Letter," and of the shy reserve with which he bore himself in society.

MR. CURTIS' REMINISCENCES.

During Hawthorne's first year's residence in Concord, I had driven up, with some friends, to an æsthetic tea at Mr. Emerson's. It was in the winter, and a

great wood-fire blazed upon the hospitable hearth.
There were various men and women assembled,
and I, who listened attentively to all the fine things
that were said, was for some time scarcely aware of
a man who sat upon the edge of the circle, a little
withdrawn, his head slightly thrown forward upon
his breast, and his bright eyes clearly burning under
his black brow. As I drifted down the stream of
talk, this person, who sat silent as a shadow, looked
to me as Webster might have looked, had he been a
poet,—a kind of poetic Webster. He rose and
walked to the window, and stood quietly there for a
long time, watching the dead white landscape. No
appeal was made to him, nobody looked after him,
the conversation flowed steadily on as if every one
understood that his silence was to be respected. It
was the same thing at table. In vain the silent man
imbibed æsthetic tea. Whatever fancies it inspired
did not flower at his lips. But there was a light in
his eye which assured me that nothing was lost. So
supreme was his silence that it presently engrossed
me to the exclusion of everything else. There was
very brilliant discourse, but this silence was much
more poetic and fascinating. Fine things were said
by the philosophers, but much finer things were implied by the dumbness of this gentleman, with heavy
brows and black hair. When he presently rose and
went, Emerson, with the "slow wise smile" that
breaks over his face, like day over the sky, said:

"Hawthorne rides well his horse of the night."

Thus he remained in my memory a shadow, a phantom, until more than a year afterward, when I came to live in Concord. Every day I passed his house, but when the villagers, thinking perhaps that I had some clue to the mystery, said:

"Do you know this Mr. Hawthorne?"

I said, "No," and trusted to time.

Time justified my confidence, and one day I too went down the avenue, and disappeared in the house. I mounted those mysterious stairs to that apocryphal study. I saw the cheerful coat of paint and golden-tinted paper-hangings, lighting up the small apartment; while the shadow of a willow-tree, that swept against the overhanging eaves, attempered the cheery western sunshine. I looked from the little northern window whence the old pastor watched the battle, and in the small dining-room beneath it upon the first floor, there was

"Dainty chicken, snow-white bread,"

and the golden juices of Italian vineyards, which still feast insatiable memory.

Our author occupied the Old Manse for three years. During that time he was not seen, probably, by more than a dozen of the villagers. His walks could easily avoid the town, and upon the river he was always sure of solitude It was his favorite habit to bathe every evening in the river, after nightfall, and in that part of it over which the old bridge stood, at which the battle was fought. Sometimes, but rarely, his boat accompanied another up the stream, and I recall the silent and preternatural vigor with which, on one occasion, he wielded his paddle to counteract the bad rowing of a friend who conscientiously considered it his duty to do something, and not let Hawthorne work alone, but who with every stroke neutralized all Hawthorne's efforts. I suppose he would have struggled until he fell senseless, rather than ask his friend to desist. His principle seemed to be, if a man cannot understand without talking to him, it is quite useless to talk, because it is immaterial whether such a man understands or not. His own sympathy was so broad and sure, that although nothing had been said for hours, his companion knew that not a thing had escaped his eye, nor had a single pulse of beauty in the day, or scene, or society, failed to thrill his heart. In this way his silence was most social. Everything seemed to have been said. It was a Barmecide feast of discourses, from which a greater satisfaction resulted than from an actual banquet.

When a formal attempt was made to desert this style of conversation, the result was ludicrous. Once Emerson and Thoreau arrived to pay a call. They were shown into the little parlor upon the avenue, and Hawthorne presently entered. Each of the guests sat upright in his chair like a Roman

Senator. To them Hawthorne seemed like a Dacian king. The call went on, but in a most melancholy manner. The host sat perfectly still, or occasionally propounded a question, which Thoreau answered accurately, and there the thread broke short off. Emerson delivered sentences that only needed the setting of an essay to charm the world; but the whole visit was a vague ghost of the Monday Evening Club at Mr. Emerson's,—it was a great failure. Had they all been lying idly by the river-bank, or strolling in Thoreau's blackberry pastures, the result would have been utterly different. But imprisoned in the proprieties of a parlor, each a wild man in his way, with a necessity of talking inherent in the nature of the occasion, there was only a waste of treasure. This was the only "call" in which I ever knew Hawthorne to be involved.

In his personal appearance, Hawthorne was not only remarkably handsome, but he looked the man of genius in every feature. His pictures hardly do him justice. "It was impossible," says Fields, " for art to give the light and beauty of his wonderful eyes. I remember to have heard, in the literary circles of Great Britain, that since Burns no author had appeared there with a finer face than Hawthorne's. I happened to be in London with Hawthorne during his consular residence in England, and was always delighted at the rustle of admiration his personal appearance excited when he entered a room. His bearing was modestly grand, and his voice touched the ear like a melody."

Once, while Hawthorne was surveyor at the port of Salem, two Shakers, leaders in their community, visited the custom-house, and were conducted through its various departments. With what keen scrutiny the broad-hatted strangers were regarded by Hawthorne, as they passed through his room, may be imagined from the fact that no sooner was the door shut as they passed out, than the elder of the celibates asked, with great interest, who that man was, and remarking upon his strong face and those eyes, the most wonderful he had ever beheld, he said, "Mark my words, that man will make in some way a deep impression upon the world."

## CHAPTER XI.

### WALT WHITMAN.

Whitman among the Bohemians of New York—His friends and associates in Pfaff's restaurant—Reminiscences of a visit to Whitman by M. D. Conway—Appearance and personal characteristics.

OF Whitman in his early days, before he became famous, and when he was only known as a "good fellow" among that wild set of Bohemians who, a generation ago, constituted the literary society of New York,—of the Whitman of those days an interesting glimpse is afforded in the following article, contributed by "Jay Charlton" to the *Danbury News*, upon

### BOHEMIANS IN AMERICA.

In the fall of 1858 a little, thin, wiry man, with a grim, weird face, and a snap of the terrier about him, made himself conspicuous among the undergraduates in literature in New York. He was assertive, quirkish, and odd, full of French jerks and Yankee quips. His face was small, hard, and cold, covered over with a forbidding beard of a dark-reddish color. He was a native of Nantucket and a graduate of Paris Bohemianism, and when he talked it was like snapping glass under your heel. He had the greatest sort of contempt for any writer who would use a word of two or more syllables when the same meaning could be conveyed in one syllable. This man's name was Henry Clapp, Jr. He believed it to be his destiny to establish a new sort of literature in New York, something that would become national, and that would cut off from all newspaper and magazine articles the long Norman words, and keep all utterances confined to the short, expressive Saxon. With this object in view he drew around him many of the promising literary men of the day. Pfaff's restaurant on Broadway, a few doors east of where it now is, near the Grand Central Hotel, was selected as the headquarters where the genial company met, and very soon "Pfaff's" had a national reputation. There was a long table under the sidewalk at which about thirty persons could seat themselves comfortably. A look in any evening after six o'clock would discover at that table Henry Clapp, Walt Whitman, Fitz James O'Brien, Ned Wilkins, George Arnold, Sheppard, Gardette, William Winter, and several others whose names I now forget. After dinner, which was always as good as one at Delmonico's, clay pipes and literary criticism were in order. Whitman generally had a half-written "yawp"—that's what he called a short poem—to submit to us. His small blue eyes would beam with good-nature, and his big, shaggy head and beard would assert themselves with a strength and grandeur that became a great poet. Walt liked to be considered a poet, but his "yawps" were wretched failures, and every publisher refused to print them until Clapp started his weekly *Press* in 1859. It was a bright paper, but of short duration. It was started without a dollar and died without a cent. William Winter was its literary critic. He was assisted by Clapp, Ada Clare, Ned Wilkins, and George Arnold, with three quarts of beer, which Clapp carried into the sanctum at No. 8 Spruce Street every afternoon in a tin pail. Turning to me in Pfaff's one cold night, while "spiced rum" seemed in great demand, Walt Whitman said, "The reason I like to drive a stage-coach on Broadway, I feel that the strength of the horses passes into my veins, my muscles, and after that I can give strength to my poetry." Walt had a great admiration for everything big, whether animate or inanimate. He thought he could write great poems if he were on the top of the Sierras or among the great trees of California. The way he came to consider himself a poet was due to a prose sketch he wrote, describing a death in a school-room. The

piece was vividly written and widely copied. That
was when he and Joe Otterson (to be remembered
as the "Bayard" of *Wilkes' Spirit of the Times*)
were setting type in a New York printing-office.
Walt was elated at the success of his sketch. Joe
told Walt that both should go to Fowler's and have
their heads phrenologically examined. They went.
Fowler told Walt that his love of approbation made
him a laughing-stock. Fowler told Joe that he was
as stubborn as a jackass, and he dismissed them
both as a pair of donkeys. But Joe was no donkey,
and he has served journalism well. Walt went to
New Orleans, was a reporter and failed. Joe went
on the *Tribune*, and was a success as night editor.
He now oscillates between a fat berth in the custom-house and the newspapers about Printing
House Square. I once saw Joe mad. When he
was doing the theatres for the *Spirit*, it was his custom to drop into Pfaff's occasionally with Ada Clif-
ton on his arm. Somebody put it in the papers that
Joe and Ada were affianced, and gave as one of the
reasons, that Joe had lately had a new coat of dye
put on his head and whiskers. He came into Pfaff's
with a scowl on his brow, and after denouncing all
the scribes round the festive board in a volley of
invectives, he left "Bohemia," to scourge its vota-
ries for years afterward with a pen "dipped in
gall."

When Fitz-Greene Halleck came up from the

state of Connecticut once or twice in the year, it was his wont to call in and see the "young fellows," as he called us. Some called him Bozzaris, and some, for short, would hail him as Marco. He laughed and took everything good-humoredly. He was pleasant and jovial as a young man of twenty. He liked a hot whiskey punch, very hot. Sitting by his side one evening that he surprised us with a visit, he ordered a hot whiskey. He would take a sip or two and then say, "Young man, this is rather cold; I want it hotter." Before he finished his punch he had it made "hotter" three times. He said to us, "When I die I shall have no literary reputation to leave behind me. What I have written has been for pastime, not for fame or money." I said, "Your Marco Bozzaris will live." His answer was, "It may, till something better takes its place. I wrote that poem with blood at fever-heat, and gave it three sittings." It was the general expression of hope round the table, after several rounds of drinks, that Astor would open his heart and increase Marco's pension from the paltry $500 which he received, to at least $5000 a year. But Halleck would laugh, shake his head, and declare himself entirely happy and satisfied. He said that Walt Whitman ought to write his "yawps" seated on an elephant, in order to add to their strength and heaviness. Walt's poetry Halleck considered no poetry at all. Yet there was and still is enough of the poetic fibre in Walt Whitman's poetry to make a half-dozen of poetic fledglings. The trouble with Walt, he lacks art and simple dignity of expression. His Pegasus is a mad bull, dashing furiously into swamps, ditches, and dung-hills, and then frightening literature by shaking his muddy horns at it. He is a man possessing a large heart, a large soul, and a large nature, but he would have served the world better had he stuck to the printer's case and left poetry alone.

At the outbreak of the Southern rebellion Walt Whitman and George Arnold came to an unpleasantness while enjoying their usual after-dinner punch. They were sitting opposite each other at the table. George was for rebellion and Walt was opposed. George was full of "treasonism" and Walt was full of "patriotism." Words grew hot. Walt warned George to be more guarded in his sentiments. George fired up more and more. Walt passed his "mawler" toward George's ear. George passed a bottle of claret toward the top-knot of the poet's head. Pfaff made a jump and gave a yell of "Oh! mine gots, mens, what's you do for dis?" Clapp broke his black pipe while pulling at Arnold's coot-tail; Ned Wilkins lost the power of his lungs for five minutes after tugging at the brawny arm of Walt; and we all received a beautiful mixture of rum, claret, and coffee on the knees of our trousers. Everything was soon amicably settled, and Walt and George shook hands, and wondered much that they were so foolish. In those days Walt dressed somewhat in the fashion of a brigand. He had a big collar to his shirt which never knew starch. That collar was rolled away back and down on his neck, which was bare nearly to the breast, which was very hairy. A black neckerchief, tied sailor-fashion, fell loosely under his collar. He wore a close-fitting monkey-jacket, which gave him a piratical cast; and a great big black slouch hat, with an immense brim and an immense crown, covered the poet's head. He gave me his picture once. I think it was taken in his shirt-sleeves. I gave it, two days afterward, to James T. Brady, while Charles G. Halpine and I were lunching with him at lower Delmonico's. Brady was the best Bohemian I ever knew. He was a genius; he loved genius. He despised wealth, and he hated work. He seemed always to be forced into work to save his friends, not to earn a livelihood. But a truce here. His memory is sacred to me. William Winter came from the Cambridge (Mass.) *Chronicle* in 1859. He wrote his poem of the "Ruined Man" while sipping a glass of mulberry wine down-stairs in a saloon in Sudbury Street, Boston. He had only twenty-five cents in his pocket to face the world. So he

> "Drank to the woman who wrought his woe,
> In the diamond morn of long ago."

Winter is considered not only one of the best dramatic writers in the country, but one of the sweetest poets—one of the few poets who know what poetry is and can write it. He can make a better after-dinner speech than any other man in New York. He is humorous, witty, and full of amusement. At Pfaff's he would have his companions almost rolling under the table with laughter, when the fit was on him to make "a few remarks."

The Rev. Moncure D. Conway, writing to the *Fortnightly Review*, in 1865, contributes the following reminiscences of

### A VISIT TO WALT WHITMAN.

Having occasion to visit New York soon after the appearance of Walt Whitman's book, I was engaged by some friends to search him out, and make some report to them concerning him. It was on a Sunday in midsummer that I journeyed through the almost interminable and monstrous streets which stretch out upon "fish-shaped Paumanok," and the direction led me to the very last house outward from the great city—a small wooden house of two stories. At my third knock a fine-looking old lady opened the door just enough to eye me carefully and ask what I wanted. It struck me, after a little, that his mother—for so she declared herself—was apprehensive that an agent of the police might be after her son on account of his audacious book. At last, however, she pointed to an open common with a central hill and told me I should find her son there. The day was excessively hot, the thermometer at nearly 100°, and the sun blazed down as only on sandy Long Island can the sun blaze. The common had not a single tree as shelter, and it seemed to me that only a devout fire-worshipper indeed could be found there on such a day. No human being could I see at first in any direction; but just as I was about to return I saw, stretched upon his back and gazing up straight at the terrible sun, the man I was seeking. With his gray clothing, his blue-gray shirt, his iron-gray hair, his swart sunburnt face and bare neck, he lay upon the brown-and-white grass—for the sun had burnt away its greenness—and was so like the earth upon which he rested, that he seemed almost enough a part of it for one to pass by without recognition. I approached him, gave my name and reason for searching him out, and asked him if he did not find the sun rather hot. "Not at all too hot," was the reply; and he confided to me that this was one of his favorite places and attitudes for composing poems. He then walked with me to his house, and took me along its narrow ways to his room. A small room of about fifteen feet square, with a single window looking out on the barren solitude of the island; a small cot, a wash-stand with a little looking-glass hung over it from a tack in the wall, a pine table with pen, ink, and paper on it, an old line-engraving, representing Bacchus, hung on the wall, and opposite a similar one of Silenus ; these constituted the visible environment of Walt Whitman. There was not, apparently, a single book in the room. In reply to my expression of a desire to see his books he declared that he had very few. I found, upon further inquiry, that he had received only such a good English education as every American lad may receive from the public schools, and that he now had access to the libraries of some of his friends. The books he seemed to know and love best were the Bible, Homer, and Shakespeare ; these he owned, and probably had in his pockets while we were talking. He had two studies where he read : one was the top of an omnibus, and the other a small mass of sand, then entirely uninhabited, far out in the ocean, called Coney Island. Many days had he passed on that island, as completely alone as Crusoe. He had no literary acquaintance, beyond a company of Bohemians who wrote for the *Saturday Press*—the organ at that time of all the audacity of New York,—whom he now and then met at Pfaff's lager-beer cellar. He was remarkably taciturn, however, about himself—considering the sublime egoism of his book—and cared only about his "poems," of which he read me one that had not then appeared. I could not help suspecting

that he must have had masters ; but he declared
that he had learned all that he knew from omnibus-
drivers, ferry-boat pilots, fishermen, boatmen, and
the men and women of the markets and wharves.
These were all inarticulate poets, and he interpreted
them. The only distinguished contemporary he
ever met was the Rev. Henry Ward Beecher, of
Brooklyn, who had visited him. He had, he said,
asked Mr. Beecher what were his feelings when he
heard a man swear, and that gentleman having admitted that he felt shocked, he (Whitman) concluded that he still preferred keeping to the boatmen for his company. He was at the time a little
under forty years of age. His father had been a
farmer on Long Island, and Walt had worked on the
farm in early life. His father was of English, his
mother of Dutch descent, thus giving him the blood
of both the races that had settled in New York. In
his youth he had listened to the preaching of the
great Quaker iconoclast, Elias Hicks, of whom his
parents were followers ; and I fancy that Hicks,
than whom few abler men have appeared in any
country in modern times, gave the most important
contribution to his education. After leaving his
father's farm, he taught school for a short time, then
became a printer, and afterward a carpenter. When
his first volume appeared, he was putting up frame
buildings in Brooklyn ; the volume was, however,
set in type entirely by his own hand. He had been

originally of the Democratic party; but when the Fugitive Slave Law was passed he found that he was too really democratic for that, and uttered his declaration of independence in a poem called "Blood-money,"—a poem not found in his works, but which was the first he ever wrote. He confessed to having no talent for industry, and that his forte was "loafing and writing poems"; he was poor, but had discovered that he could, on the whole, live magnificently on bread and water. He had travelled through the country as far as New Orleans, where he had once edited a paper. But I would find, he said, all of him—his life, works, and days—in his book; he had kept nothing back whatever.

We passed the remainder of the day roaming or "loafing" on Staten Island, where we had shade and many miles of a beautiful beach. Whilst we bathed, I was impressed by a certain grandeur about the man, and remembered the picture of Bacchus on the wall of his room. I then perceived that the sun had put a red mask on his face and neck, and that his body was a ruddy blonde, pure and noble, his form being at the same time remarkable for fine curves and for that grace of movement which is the flower of shapely and well-knit bones. His head was uniform in every way; his hair, which was strongly mixed with gray, was cut close to his head, and, with his beard, was in strange contrast to the almost infantile fulness and serenity of his face. This serenity, however, came from the quiet, light-blue eyes, and above these there were three or four horizontal furrows, which life had ploughed. The first glow of any kind which I saw about him was when he entered the water, which he fairly hugged with a lover's enthusiasm. But when he was talking about that which deeply interested him, his voice, always gentle and clear, became slow, and his eyelids had a tendency to decline over his eyes. It was impossible not to feel at every moment the *reality* of every word and movement of the man, and also the surprising delicacy of one who was even freer with his pen than modest Montaigne.

After making an appointment to meet Walt again during the week, when we would saunter through the streets of New York, I went off to find myself almost sleepless with thinking of this new acquaintance. He had so magnetized me, so charged me, as it were, with somewhat undefinable, that for a time the only wise course of life seemed to be to put on a blue shirt and a blouse and loaf about Manahatta and Paumanok—"loaf and invite my soul," to use my new friend's phrase. I found time hanging heavily on my hands, and the sights of the brilliant city tame, whilst waiting for the next meeting, and wondered if he would seem such a grand fellow when I saw him again. I found him on the appointed morning setting in type, in a Brooklyn printing-office, a paper from the *Democratic Review*, urging the superiority of Walt Whitman's poetry over that of Tennyson, which he meant to print (as he did every thing, *pro* and *con*, in full) in the appendix of his next edition. He still had on the workingman's garb, which (he said) he had been brought up to wear, and now found it an advantage to continue. It became plain to me as I passed along the streets and on the ferry with him, that he was a prince incognito amongst his lower-class acquaintances. They met him continually, grasped his hand with enthusiasm, and laughed and chatted (but on no occasion did he laugh, nor, indeed, did I ever see him smile). Having some curiosity to know whether this class of persons appreciated him at all, I privately said to a workman in corduroys, with whom I had seen him conversing, and whom he had just left : " Do you know who that man there is ? " " That be Walt Whitman." "Have you known him long ? " " Many a year." " What sort of a man is he ? " " A fus'-rate man is Walt. Nobody knows Walt but likes him ; nearly everybody knows him and—and *loves* him." There was a curious look about the fellow as he emphasized the word *loves*, as if he were astonished at the success with which he had expressed himself. " He has written a book, has n't he ? " " Not as ever I hearn on." Several times as we were crossing the waters about New York, I was able to separate from him and put similar questions to artisans and others with whom I had seen him interchange greetings or words; but I found none of them knew any thing about his writings, though all felt a pride in being acquainted with him. Nothing could surpass the blending of *insouciance* with active observation in his manner as we strolled along the streets. "Look at that face!" he exclaimed once as we paused near the office of the *Herald*. I looked, and beheld a boy of perhaps fifteen years, with certainly a hideous countenance, the face one-sided, and one eye almost hanging out of a villainous low forehead. He had a bundle under his arm. "There," said Walt, "is a New York reptile. There's poison about his fangs, I think." We watched him as he looked furtively about, and presently he seemed to see that we had our eyes on him, and was skulking off. At that my companion beckoned to him, and after a little succeeded in bringing him to us, when we found that he was selling obscene books. At the Tombs prison we went among the prisoners, and the confidence and volubility with which they ran to him to pour out their grievances, as if he were one in authority, was singular. In one man's case he took a special interest. The man, pending trial for a slight offence, had been put into a very disagreeable and unhealthy place. Hearing his account, Walt turned about, went straight to the governor of the prison, and related the matter—ending thus, "In my opinion it is a damned shame." The governor was at first stunned by this in an outsider, and one in the dress of a laborer, then he eyed him from head to foot as if questioning whether to commit him; during which the offender stood eying the governor in turn with a severe serenity. Walt triumphed in this duel of eye-shots, and, without another word, the governor called an officer to go and transfer the prisoner to a better room. I have often remembered the oath of Walt Whitman on this occasion as being one of the most religious utterances I have ever heard.

Henry Thoreau visited Walt Whitman in 1856; and I find in his posthumous "Letters" edited by R. W. Emerson, two that were addressed to the poet, giving him good advice in the matter of reading, and especially, it would seem, answering some questions about Oriental books. In another letter, written by Thoreau to a friend soon after the visit to which I have referred, he says, "That Walt Whitman, of whom I wrote to you, is the most interesting fact to me at present. I have just read his second edition (which he gave me), and it has done me more good than any reading for a long time. There are two or three pieces in the book which are disagreeable, simply sensual. It is as if the beasts spoke. Of course Walt Whitman can communicate to us no experience, and if we are shocked, whose experience is it that we are reminded of? * * * He occasionally suggests something a little more than human. Wonderfully like the Orientals, too, considering that when I asked him if he had read them, he said, 'No : tell me about them.' He is apparently the greatest democrat the world has seen."

## CHAPTER XII.

### BAYARD TAYLOR.

Prof. Boyesen's reminiscences—Taylor's wonderful memory—His frankness and cheerfulness—Various anecdotes—His last days.

In a paper written for *Lippincott's Magazine* shortly after the death of the poet-traveller, Prof. Hjalmar H. Boyesen contributed the following

#### REMINISCENCES OF BAYARD TAYLOR.

It was in October, 1873, that I saw Bayard Taylor for the first time. He was then staying with his brother-in-law in Gotha, but paid frequent visits to Leipsic for the purpose of examining the famous collection of Goethe editions and manuscripts then belonging to the publisher Salomon Hirzel, but recently bequeathed by him to the library of the University of Leipsic. I too had a letter of introduction to Herr Hirzel, and cherished a vague hope that he would, after some preliminary remarks on my part, volunteer to show me his Goethe treasures.

Ever faithfully yours
Bayard Taylor

In this, however, I was disappointed. He evidently chose to look upon my interest in his great countryman as youthful eccentricity. I had no gray hairs as yet, nor was I bald ; how, then, could I know any thing about Goethe?

Der amerikanische Dichter, Taylor, he remarked *en passant*, was at present studying the collection with much care, and meant in time to publish the results of his investigations. Without further parleying I took my leave, and met a gentleman who had been pointed out to me as Bayard Taylor, on the sidewalk about fifty steps from the house. I had a strong temptation to introduce myself, but lacked courage. I thought of Hans Christian Andersen's unhappy experience when he introduced himself to Jacob Grimm.

In the autumn of the following year (1874) I met Mr. Taylor at the Century Club in New York, where, in a corner which in time will become historic, he sat surrounded by his friends E. C. Stedman, R. H. Stoddard, S. S. Conant, and A. R. MacDonough. A few months later Mr. Taylor delivered a course of lectures on German literature at Cornell University, and I then had the privilege of daily association with him. We spent long evenings together on the piazza of a common friend, whence a magnificent view stretches northward over the broad green valley and the glorious lake. We smoked many a peaceful cigar, discussing all the while our common European experiences and indulging in desultory praise or criticism of brother authors. I then discovered for the first time the enormous retentive power of Mr. Taylor's memory. He could quote by the hour English, German, Italian, and even Swedish poetry, and apparently have inexhaustible treasures still in reserve. I remember on one occasion we were debating the merits of the various translations of Tegnér's "Frithjof's Saga," and I was maintaining that after Mr. Longfellow's exquisite rendering of "The Temptation" and a few other separate poems, no poetaster who chose to translate the whole work had any right to try his unskilled hand on these, but ought simply to incorporate Mr. Longfellow's renderings—of course with proper acknowledgment of their source. "And still," I added, "there is in single passages of the original a flavor so subtle that even so sensitive an artist as Longfellow fails to catch it. It is so fleeting that it utterly refuses to be transferred into another tongue."

And I began to quote:

Strax är gamle kungen vaken: " Myeket var den sömn mig väd;
Ljufligt sofver man i skuggan, skyddad af den tappres svärd—

Here my memory failed me, and Mr. Taylor promptly continued:

Dock hoor är ditt svärd, o främling? blixtens broder, hvar är han?

Hvem hor skilt er, I som aldrig skulla skiljas fran hvarann?"
and so on for five or six verses.

I have frequently heard Mr. Taylor complain that his memory was an inconvenience to him. He would read by chance some absurd or absolutely colorless verse, and it would continue to haunt him for days. One single reading sometimes sufficed to fix a poem indelibly in his mind. The first part of "Faust" I verily believe he could repeat from beginning to end; at all events, I never happened to allude to any passage which he could not recite at a moment's notice. Even the second part, with its evasive and impalpable meanings, he had partly committed to memory; or, rather, it had, without any effort of his own, committed itself to his memory.

Many of my friends who enjoyed the privilege of associating with Bayard Taylor have similar anecdotes to relate. His fund of comic and serio-comic verse from obscure poets was a constant source of amusement to all who came in contact with him. The poet Chivers, for instance—what wonderful things he has produced! and how soon, but for Taylor, his ungrateful country would have forgotten him!

Two years later, when he was again lecturing at Cornell, he paid me a visit in my study, and after some preliminary conversation asked me to show him my manuscripts. I readily complied, and placed before him a large roll of papers, which he took up and began to inspect.

"What is this?" he exclaimed—"apparently a life of Goethe and Schiller!"

I replied that it was merely scattered reflections, lecture-notes, and excerpts from books relating to the two German poets, and that in time I hoped to be able to arrange them into a connected biography.

"But, my dear boy," he cried, "don't you know that you are stealing my thunder?"

I replied that I did not know that he was engaged in the same work, and if I had known it I should not flatter myself with the belief that I could compete with him.

"Ah, that is all very nice and modest," he said, smiling, "but if you don't think you can compete with me or anybody under the sun, you should not be in a hurry about publishing your biography. Listen to me, and I will propose an arrangement to you. I have collected almost every thing that has been written about Goethe and Schiller, and I have several of the original editions. Your Goethe library, although it is good as far as it goes, is, judging by appearances, rather incomplete. Now, the next time you go to New York you can come to me and select whatever books you may want, and keep them as long as you need them. If there is any thing you need before then, only let me know and I shall send it to you. No two men who labor earnestly in a good cause can interfere with each other, and the more there is written about Goethe the better for me. It will prepare the public for the fact that Goethe's literary and scientific activity has a universal significance, and that the riddle of his life has as yet not been properly solved. Lewes' entertaining apology, in my opinion, hardly deserves the name of a biography."

From this time forth I remained in constant communication with Bayard Taylor, and the subject of our conversation and correspondence was almost invariably Goethe. If in the course of my German reading I discovered a characteristic anecdote of the great poet, I hastened to call his attention to it; but I need not say that I was the recipient of such favors much more frequently than I bestowed them. Whenever I visited New York—which I did about every other month—we spent the most delightful evenings together in his library, discussing the subject of our common enthusiasm. During the last two years, while he was engaged in writing "Prince Deukalion," he never failed to read to me, in his splendidly sonorous voice, the last act he had finished, and this naturally furnished material for the discussion of many social and religious problems. It must be evident to every one that he has in his poem attempted to define his social and poetic creed, and the hopeful and sanguine element of his character has there found its most complete expression. He endeavored, above all, to avoid dogmatism in his statement of his convictions, and to make his imagery so ample and expressive that it should hint at the philosophic truth, as a loose and gracefully flowing garment suggests, and by its general outline reveals, the form of the man within. I think he was himself astonished at the ease with which he wrote; as soon as he was tuned up to a certain key the rhymes came of themselves, and a throng of ideas whirled through his mind, each clamoring for expression. The dogmatic rock which, at the outset, he was inclined to fear, was easily cleared: at the beginning of the last act, however, he came to a stand-still, and laid the poem aside for about six months. At the end of that time two different conclusions had suggested themselves to him, and he had some difficulty in deciding between them. My recollection of the rejected plan is so vague that I shall not venture even to sketch it.

What especially impressed itself upon my memory on these occasions was the undisguised delight of the poet in his own work. His mental perceptions were so delicate that he felt in an instant whether I was *en rapport* with him, and it was useless before him to feign admiration.

"Now," he would say, looking up quickly from his manuscript, "you have some objection to that, haven't you?"

"I simply didn't catch your meaning," I would

answer. "If you will allow me to read the passage myself, I don't doubt I shall grasp the thought."

One evening I found upon his table a fresh magazine which I had not yet seen containing some productions of mi      I seized it, perhaps a little eagerly, and glanced furtively at a certain page which particularly interested me.

"Ah," he cried, laughing, "I see you have not yet got over the first joy of seeing your thoughts temporarily immortalized in the monthly magazines."

I confessed that I was not yet a stranger to the feeling he had described.

"And I will make you a confession in return," he said. "I have been a writer now for more than thirty years, and yet I have not entirely conquered that first youthful delight. I really believe that the first glance at a printed page of mine, and especially at the first sight of a new book of mine, will never lose their delightful novelty to me if I live to be a hundred years old."

People who knew Bayard Taylor but superficially were apt to accuse him of what they were pleased to call literary vanity. To me this charge seems to be based upon an imperfect comprehension of the rare simplicity and earnestness of the man. Of course he believed in himself and in his own poetic mission, and he was not disposed to admit into the circle of his more intimate friends any one who questioned the genuineness of his poetic talent. But who likes to have his merits questioned in his own presence? and who chooses his friends among his hostile critics? It is not to be denied that the conventional code of etiquette requires that a man should deprecate his own worth, and, especially in the case of an author, that he should put a very modest estimate upon his own productions. Bayard Taylor was too frank and honest to conform to this rule. If you told him that you thought his "Pæan to the Dawn" in the "Songs of the Orient" was a wonderful poem, his fine eyes would light up with pleasure, and he would describe to you in vivid colors the situation which had suggested the song to him. If you marvelled at the skill in the management of difficult metres which he had displayed in this or that passage of "Faust," he never answered, "Oh, that is nothing," or, "Do you think that so remarkable?" but he exclaimed with the emphasis of conviction, "I am glad you give me credit for having done it well. It was by no means a happy inspiration: it was the result of hard and honest labor. I had rejected no less than seven versions before I found the one you admire."

Once, as I came to return half a dozen commentaries on "Faust" which I had borrowed from Bayard Taylor, I found him in his library chuckling to himself over a letter which he was writing. "Listen to this," he said, after having extended to me his hand for a cordial grasp. "Isn't it delicious? Here is a man in —— who writes to me in absolute earnest, asking me to compose an oration for him which he is to deliver as his own on a certain public occasion."

He began to read, and I cannot resist the temptation to quote the letter from memory:

"Mr. Bayard Taylor:

"Dear Sir: Understanding that you are a poet of some note, I write to you to ask you your prices for writing orations for public occasions. I have been requested by my fellow-citizens to make a speech of about an hour on the —— ——, and, as I have not time to prepare it to my satisfaction, I thought you might write it for me to memorize. Please send on your prices, and oblige

"Yours truly,
"X. X."

Taylor answered in a strain of mock-seriousness, and if my memory serves me right his letter ran approximately as follows:

"Mr. X. X.:

"Dear Sir: Your favor of the —— inst. received. I should take great pleasure in complying with your request, but regret that the press of business compels me to decline. The Presidential campaign [1876], and the onerous duties it imposes upon men of my line of business, absorb all my time and energy. I have at present no less than twenty-eight campaign orations to write—eighteen Democratic and ten Republican—and fresh orders are daily arriving. Add to this five temperance speeches, three funeral orations, and creeds and a complete doctrinal system for a new sect just to be established, and you will, no doubt, comprehend that I am justified in declining further engagements. My price is usually $18.35 per thousand words, but owing to the great rush of business I have recently raised to $27.47.

"In conclusion, allow me to recommend to you my friends Mr. E. C. Stedman, No. —— —— Street, and Mr. R. H. Stoddard, No. —— —— Street, either of whom, I have no doubt, would be willing and competent to supply exactly the kind of oration which you want.

"Very truly yours,
"BAYARD TAYLOR."

I shall not attempt to give any detailed account of my intercourse with Bayard Taylor during the time that intervened between this incident and my meeting with him in Berlin in August, 1878. He had then just returned from a brief sojourn in the Thüringerwald, where his family were still staying. He had volunteered to look over the revised proof of my "Goethe and Schiller," and it was this promise which had induced me to select the unpicturesque Berlin as my first stopping-place. I found him the same warm-hearted and sympathetic friend as always, but, seeing that his appearance had undergone some change which might be attributable to illness, I hesitated to present my proof-sheets. He did not feel quite well, he acknowledged, but a little rest and dieting would soon restore him to perfect health. What he particularly regretted was that his indisposition prevented him from attacking his biography of Goethe, for which he had been collecting

The Homestead, Chester Co Penn.

materials for so many years. He was burning with impatience to commit the first chapter to paper. Then he should feel at least that he was fairly started, and the continuation of the work would be a matter of course. It was unfortunate that the book had been so much talked about while it was yet in the embryonic state, and he had always taken occasion to contradict the statement, so frequently made by the American newspapers, that he had been sent to Germany in order that he might have an opportunity of writing it. After all this talk people naturally expected something very extraordinary, and he did not doubt that when the work finally saw the light the great majority of readers would be disappointed. They would not be prepared to accept his view of Goethe, because they did not possess the culture necessary for a proper estimation of his worth. To the student who was familiar with the spirit of the German language and people he meant to make his conclusions inevitable. His book would have nothing in common with that of Lewes except, of course, the necessary reference to the same facts. He then related an anecdote, which I have printed once before, but which may bear repeating: Some years ago (in 1874, if I am not mistaken) Bayard Taylor called on Thomas Carlyle, and after having communicated to him his intention of writing a life of Goethe, asked him for an account of his own epistolary intercourse with the poet. Carlyle sat for a moment pondering, then looking up abruptly he said in a slow and emphatic tone, "That man, sir, was my salvation."

Frequently on fine afternoons Mr. Taylor would cause a profound sensation in the unfashionable little street where my wife and I had established our Bohemian head-quarters. Whenever his fine carriage, drawn by two stately horses (which, he confessed to me privately, he hired by the month), rolled away over the uneven cobble-stones, a congregation of female heads would appear, scattered at irregular intervals over the façades of the tall stone buildings, and four or five self-commissioned messengers would come thundering on our door, announcing with breathless excitement, "Seine Excellenz, der amerikanische Minister." I felt that we rose immensely in the estimation of our Teutonic neighbors after each of these visits, and when Mr. Taylor was seen descending the stairs with my wife on his arm and politely helping her into the carriage, our landlady made a rash wager of twenty-five cents with the man who furnished our dinners that we belonged to the American nobility. When we disclaimed any such honor she consoled herself with the reflection that for some important reason we travelled incognito. "Great people often did," she was heard to observe to her antagonist, who daily insisted upon the payment of the wager.

During these drives through the long green avenues of the Thiergarten, Mr. Taylor was always in his happiest humor.

"I feel like a boy who has unexpectedly got a long vacation," he exclaimed one day as we seated ourselves in the carriage. "I have had a horrible fear, and to-day for the first time I can breathe freely."

On inquiring what had caused his fear he continued: "You know I had begun to attribute all the pain and discomfort from which I have been suffering of late to some disorder of the kidneys, and I have always had a mortal dread of kidney diseases. Now my doctor assures me, after a thorough examination, that that organ is perfectly sound, and that my disorder is a simple catarrh of the stomach. This piece of intelligence lifts a stone from my breast. I assure you I have n't been so happy for many a day."

I should not venture to report our conversations on these occasions in their chronological order, but a great many incidents of Bayard Taylor's foreign experience still survive in my memory with a subdued accompaniment of song of birds, glinting sunshine, and gentle rustling of leaves. I then know that they were first told me during one of our drives in the Thiergarten. Thus, for instance, the following story, which emphatically refutes the recent assertion of one of our prominent journals that no one reads Mr. Taylor's novels: One day last summer, while Mr. Taylor was travelling southward, he observed on stepping off the train the Princess Bismarck. She beckoned to him, and after a few polite remarks informed him that her husband was on the train, and was at that moment reading a novel entitled "Joseph and his Friends." She had no doubt that he would be pleased to receive a visit from the author. Mr. Taylor accordingly announced himself, and was admitted to the special car in which the Chancellor was sitting.

The latter greeted him cordially, and invited him to take a seat at his side. "I was just reading your novel for the second time," he began, "and I like it more and more. But there is one serious mistake in it. You let your villains escape far too easily. That is not poetic justice, nor any kind of justice, in my opinion."

"I could not help thinking," remarked Taylor in relating the story to me, "that this criticism was profoundly characteristic of Bismarck."

Of Lord Beaconsfield, Mr. Taylor had rather a more favorable opinion than the majority of his countrymen. At a dinner given in honor of the members of the Berlin Congress, he met the English Premier for the first time. He was exceedingly polite, but apparently did not know Mr. Taylor in any other than his diplomatic capacity. In the course of the conversation the latter made the remark that he had known and admired Mr. Disraeli the man of letters before he had learned to admire Lord Beaconsfield the statesman : being himself a member of the literary guild, he had formerly had the honor of claiming Lord Beaconsfield as a colleague.

His lordship seemed a little puzzled at this, and did not immediately reply. "Ah," he exclaimed after a moment's reflection, "you are Bayard Taylor, who has translated "Faust" and written so many delightful books. Of course I know you very well."

During the months of September and October, Mr. Taylor's illness began to assume a more serious character. He suffered the most excruciating pains in his side, and the doctors changed the location of his disorder, and now declared that it was his colon which was affected. Nevertheless, he remained bravely sanguine, and so persistently cheerful as almost to dispel the apprehensions of his friends. "I wish," he exclaimed one day in the midst of a groan, "that this trouble with the colon would soon come—ah!—to a period."

I have especially a painfully vivid recollection of an evening I spent with him in his bedroom during the second week of October. He lay outstretched on a narrow German bed, every now and then pressing his hands violently against his side, while endeavoring to stifle a groan. I rose several times to go, thinking that my presence might cause him inconvenience. But he begged me earnestly to stay. "I want you to talk to me," he said. "Talk about any thing under the sun—about Goethe, socialism, politics, or, in fact, any thing. I am not so ill as you think, and it does not hurt me to talk."

We accordingly discussed a number of topics, among others Tourgueneff, Auerbach, Spielhagen, etc. I happened to suggest, I do not know how, that it would soon be incumbent upon Taylor to write his autobiography, as otherwise a great deal of valuable and interesting information both about himself and about other prominent men would be lost.

"I have thought of that frequently," he replied; "and if it were not for my life of Goethe I should feel tempted to go to work immediately. By the way, do you know any thing more fascinating than a great white virgin sheet of paper? It has always possessed a strong charm for me from the time I was a boy. I feel such a temptation to scribble it all over with my thoughts, which may not always enhance its value. But speaking of the autobiography, I think it would be a very easy and delightful task. I have always been in the habit of writing elaborate descriptions to my wife of whatever has happened to me during her absence, and thus a great many important incidents of my life have been chronicled. She has kept all my letters, and, as every thing is very clearly and coherently written,

I think my biographer, whether it be myself or some one else, will not encounter much difficulty in recording the latter half of my life. If only this annoying infirmity would leave me! If it were something serious, I might have some patience with it, but to have all this discomfort for the sake of a miserable colon is positively unendurable."

The fearful pun which has persisted in haunting me these many months seemed under the circumstances grave and pathetic. I smiled faintly, but I could not laugh; for I feared that the doctors, for some reason, thought it best to deceive him, and that his malady was more alarming than he imagined.

"Do you know," he resumed after a while, "Count Usedom sent me the other day a splendid mask of Goethe—not a death-mask, but one taken from the living face. It is full of character, is superbly modelled, and has the most expressive wrinkles. Ask my wife to show it to you before you go. If I could have a few copies taken of it, I should like to give you one."

"It is odd," he resumed after a while, "how deeply rooted the idea is among our people, that because a man is a good novelist he must necessarily be a bad poet or dramatist, and if he is a good poet his novels or his dramas deserve only censure. A man like Goethe, whose rich nature demanded such manifold and various expression, would never be comprehended by our reviewers. They would damn "Faust" because "Werther" had been a success. 'Now, you made such a hit with your novel,' they would say, 'why don't you stick to that in which you have excelled, instead of trying your unskilled hand on something which you don't understand?' Novel-writing, poetry, travels, the drama, are conceived to be each a separate trade, and to be a poet and a novelist at the same time is in the eyes of our critics about as anomalous as it would be to combine the practice of law and medicine or to profess equal skill in carpentry and shoemaking. The Germans have a much nobler conception of the vocation of a man of letters. If he is an imaginative writer, no matter of what kind, they call him *Dichter*, and they leave the whole field of imaginative writing at his disposal. If Paul Heyse, who began as a novelist, writes a drama or a poem, it does not in the least disturb them. So also Freytag has gained an equal success on the stage and as a writer of romances. Goethe and Schiller would have been at a loss to define their proper specialty. Their vocation was that of *Dichter*, and they selected the form which suited best the idea they wished to develop. Their occasional hesitation between two literary forms thus becomes perfectly intelligible."

I asked Mr. Taylor whether he had not a personal grievance against our reviewers for underestimating the value of his poems and persisting in extolling him in his capacity of traveller.

"I'll be frank with you," he answered, "and confess that nothing has annoyed me more than the incessant reference to me in newspapers and lecture-bills as 'Bayard Taylor, the Great Traveller.' During my last lecture-tour through the West I discovered how firmly I was lodged in the minds of the American people as a traveller: every man who introduced me made some plain allusion to my early vagabondism, and every farmer or farmer's daughter who came up to shake hands with me after the lecture informed me that he or she had read my travels 'with *so* much interest.' I often think of myself as an artist who on account of poverty was obliged to make his start in life as a bricklayer. When he had in this way gained the means to supplement his deficient culture, he began to model in clay and to make statues in marble. He would have preferred to omit altogether the discipline of bricklaying, but circumstances had compelled him to accept it: he knew from the beginning that sculpture was his proper calling. Now, if this sculptor shows himself a worthy member of the artistic guild and produces work of artistic merit, is it fair to be for ever saying to him: 'You were such an excellent bricklayer! Why didn't you continue to lay bricks?' That is exactly what the American public are continually saying to me. I haven't a particle of pride in my books of travel. They make no artistic pretension, and if I have no other title to remembrance, I shall be content to be forgotten."

At the risk of violating the chronological order I shall take the liberty to relate an incident which is recalled to me by what I have just written. Two or three years ago, when I was dining with Bayard Taylor at the house of a common friend, one of the guests present persisted in turning the conversation on sun-myths. Whatever was said served in some way as an excuse for introducing a sun-myth; history, mythology, religion, all resolved themselves into sun-myths. Bayard Taylor listened, but had hitherto contributed but little to the discussion.

"Did it ever occur to you," he said gravely, addressing himself to the myth-maker, "why the name Smith is so common in almost all countries—in Germany, England, America, and Scandinavia?"

Some one suggested that it was because the trade of blacksmith was the most indispensable among primitive nations, and that the man was named after his trade.

"Oh, no," said Mr. Taylor, still with the utmost gravity: "I don't think that accounts for it. The name Smith is obviously a contraction of Sun-myth—Sumyth, Smyth, Smith. Now, isn't that convincing?"

We all burst into a hearty laugh, and the sun-myths were temporarily dismissed. The ingenious derivation of the name which is never loved by its possessors naturally led to a discussion of etymology and the freaks of phonetic corruption. The conversation was once more in danger of assuming a too exclusively professional tone, when a happy inspiration of Mr. Taylor's again came to our rescue.

"Do you know," he said, turning to our etymologist, "what is the derivation of the word *restaurant?*"

"It is of course the Latin verb *restaurare*, ' to restore,' ' to invigorate,'" answered the latter unhesitatingly.

"No, you are quite mistaken," rejoined Taylor with a twinkle in his eye. "Restaurant is derived from *res*, 'a thing,' and *taurus*, 'a bull,'—a bully thing."

It was on the evening of October 13th that we went to take leave of our friends at the American Legation. We found Mr. Taylor in his library, seated in an easy-chair, with a shawl wrapped about his limbs. He was obliged to remain in the same position, and it was evident that every movement caused him pain. Nevertheless, his conversation was very animated, and he scattered his bright little remarks about him with his usual lavishness. He had just finished furnishing the Legation, and invited us to make the round of the rooms with Mrs. Taylor.

On our return he related a number of odd experiences he had had with German tradesmen, who could not be made to understand that there was any other way of doing a thing than the German way. Their bland stupidity was highly exasperating. He had tried to demonstrate to them that a bed ought to offer certain conveniences for repose, and that a man of his size needed a longer bed than a man of five feet eight. Nevertheless, all German beds seemed to be made on the supposition that this was the normal height of a man, and that if he were taller it was an accidental malformation which he must expect to suffer for. In ordering his beds he (Taylor) had particularly emphasized this necessity of prolonging them beyond the German "measure of a man," but all his efforts in this direction had proved futile, and now he would have to return the useless things, which would involve another battle with German prejudice and German tradition. The creed of the Teutonic cabinet-maker might be expressed as follows: "The man must be made for the bed, not the bed for the man."

As we rose to go, Mr. Taylor handed me a letter of introduction to his friend Gustav Freytag at Siebleben, near Gotha.

"I shall only say *auf Wiedersehen*," he said as he shook our hands cordially; "for of course you will be here next summer."

Those were the last words I ever heard him utter.

From the hall, where we lingered for some moments, I looked again through the half-open door at his noble, manly face. Mrs. Taylor, who had accompanied us out, confessed to us, with a little trembling in her voice, that her husband's condition was very alarming to her—that she could not be quite as sanguine as he. The doctors had now decided that he was threatened with inflammation of the liver, and that he must immediately start for the baths of Carlsbad: the waters there were a universally accepted remedy for liver complaint.

Some two months later (December 21st) we were standing on the upper balcony of the Villa Albani, outside the walls of Rome. It was a glorious sunny afternoon; the green Campagna rolled away in stately monotony toward the horizon, and the Alban Mountains defined themselves lightly, through a bluish mist, against the sky. Then an American friend entered, and on seeing me called out, "Bayard Taylor is dead!"

The scene is indelibly engraved upon my memory —the bluish mountains and the Campagna gleaming in the subdued sunshine, and the many domes looming against the sky. The name of my friend and my regret at his loss have henceforth some strange association with the classical soil and the Roman sky. It is as if I had seen him there for the last time, and there bidden him the last good-bye.

## CHAPTER XIII.

### SWINBURNE AND OSCAR WILDE.

*Anecdotes and personal sketches—Swinburne and Browning—An evening with Swinburne—Oscar Wilde—The idiosyncrasies of the London æsthete.*

MR. ALGERNON CHARLES SWINBURNE, according to an article in the *Galaxy*, contributed by a personal friend, is a member of the English aristocracy, his father, Admiral Swinburne, and his mother, Lady Jane Ashburnham, both belonging to a very exclusive set, composed of Catholics of old blood, who form a clique of their own somewhat like that of the ancient Codini family at Florence. The poet was himself educated in France, "in the Ultramontane fashion," but he seems to have bravely gotten over the influences of his early training, since he is now distinguished for his "intense hatred of established religion and moral codes." From the Ultramontane school in France he went to Oxford. While there he commenced a correspondence with Charles Baudelaire and made the acquaintance of Lord Houghton, who even then declared he had met the poet of the future. Leaving Oxford without a degree, he paid a visit to Florence, on a sort of pilgrimage to see Landor, for whom he had an enthusiastic admiration. Since his return he has lived principally in London, where he affects the companionship of artists and men of letters, and keeps himself clear of the scented crush called London society. He has not much taste, we are told, for the brainless dancing girls who fill up the English salons and who have nothing to recommend them but personal beauty, polished manners, and agile limbs. He is, nevertheless, of opinion that women are the only fit company for a man of intellect, and that old women are the best. Mr. Swinburne is a poet in character. He is not as other men are, and yet is never guilty of affecting eccentricity. He does not converse, he is either silent (it is the silence of an observer) or, like Coleridge, pours forth. When excited, his flow of language and splendor of imagery are alone sufficient to prove that he is a genius. He is willing to recite his poems before publication. His voice is monotonous, he *intones*

—but it is very earnest. Before the first series of his poems and ballads came out he kept them in a fire-proof box, in loose sheets, and, plunging his arm in up to his elbow, used to bring out his favorites. "Have you heard Sappho?" was a common question among his friends. "Sappho" was the name that "Anactoria" went by. "We did not think that he would ever dare to publish this poem with 'Dolores,' 'The Leper,'" etc.

The following curious little anecdote in regard to the poet is told by a correspondent of *Appleton's Journal.*

Having received an invitation to dinner at a certain house, he arrived in due course. It was observed that he was rather excited and strange in manner, but as he is known to have a singularly high-strung, nervous temperament, no particular attention was paid to this circumstance. Dinner went off in the usual way. The guest of the evening was particularly brilliant; his rapid, discursive conversation never ceased. After dinner, in the drawing-room, he consented to read some sonnets from his most recently published volume, and he was good enough to expound in most eloquent and luminous language the subtler meanings of these poems and their connection with each other. His audience were delighted. Here and there, of course there was a touch of extravagance in his speech, but to a poet some poetic license must be granted. Before going he requested the lady of the house to accept the volume, and inscribed her name in it. All this was very well, but some two or three days afterward he called upon his host, and immediately began to pour forth a whole string of apologies. He had mislaid the card—he had mistaken the night—he had had to go down into the country. This astonished person now discovered that his guest of the evening was absolutely in ignorance of his ever having been near the house, that he had come to apologize for having neglected the invitation, and that he was anxious that the lady of the house should accept a copy, to be sent from the publishers, of the very book which he himself had given her.

From my knowledge of the author of "Chastelard" [continues our correspondent], I have not the smallest doubt that the above story is true. Mr. Swinburne is one of the most nervous men—he is very slightly built, and not more than five feet two in height—you could possibly imagine. I shall never forget seeing him at the poetic readings given by the poet Buchanan, some years ago, in the Hanover-Square Rooms. There, in a corner, his intellectual face now wearing a scowl, now a beatific expression, as he was pleased or displeased with his brother poet's elocution, did he sit twirling his fingers and thumbs in a ludicrously excited way. Ere long he became the observed of every one. "Who is that?" whispered a mercantile friend to me, nodding toward him. "That," replied I, wishing to surprise the man of figures, "is one of our greatest poets, Mr. Swinburne." "Indeed!" was the reply. "Well, I've always heard that poets were a rum lot; now I've no doubt about it!"

Mr. Swinburne's sense of humor is deficient, and it is therefore not surprising that his ardent temperament should frequently lead him into ludicrous extravagancies. Not very long ago he excited the laughter of all England by bringing with him, to a public banquet given in honor of Robert Browning, a footstool which he insisted on placing at the master's feet and solemnly seating himself thereon. The humor of the situation was no doubt fully appreciated by the elder poet, who, in his every-day aspect, is a thoroughly common-sensible man of the world. Browning, on his side, has a warm liking for Swinburne, but he recognizes his deficiencies as well as his merits. "You foolish boy!" he is represented as saying to him on one occasion, with a playful shake of the finger, "what do you mean by prostituting such a splendid genius?"

A contributor to *Lippincott's Magazine*, who veils her personality under the transparent initials of L. C. M., gives the following description of

AN EVENING WITH SWINBURNE.

I had often heard in London society of Swinburne's matchless eloquence, but, though I had met him before, I had really formed no definite idea of him until, a few weeks ago, I passed an evening in his company, in the pleasant study of Philip Bourke Marston, the poet. There were present only Miss Marston, the two poets, and myself. Swinburne has been said by an enthusiastic literary lady of London to be "the only poet who looks like a poet." Perhaps I do not quite understand what it is to look like a poet, for I should have said that Mr. Marston equally came up to this somewhat fanciful ideal; but it is true that when Swinburne is at his best he has a wonderful look of inspiration. He is not very tall, and is rather slight than otherwise in figure. His forehead is almost disproportionately large as compared with the rest of his face. Under it glow his great, luminous eyes, uncertain in color, because for ever changing with his thoughts. His hair is of that dark red which Titian loved to paint. His complexion is fair, and his mouth rather small and extremely gentle in expression.

He had brought that evening, at Mr. Marston's

request, some of the proofs of his new volume of "Poems and Ballads," which he read to us. He prefers reading his own poetry to hearing it read by others; and certainly his reading is most characteristic. It seems, perhaps, a little mannered at first, until he gets into the swing of his own inspiration; then he takes you with him, and bears you out on the free wings of his song till you forget time and space, and sit as under a spell. I think—whatever difference of opinion may exist as to Swinburne's rank among the great poets of the world—there can be no difference of opinion as to his wonderful mastery of words and of rhythm. The sensuous delight one takes in his mere music is in itself an enchantment. And you never so feel this marvellous music as when he is reading—or rather chanting—his own words.

After the proofs had been laid aside came a discussion of Charlotte Brontë, apropos of the brilliant Brontë monograph recently published by Swinburne. In the poet's eyes, Jane Eyre has no fault. To suggest that she might have been in any wise more noble was sufficient to rouse him to passionate eloquence in her defence. But with him defence, like denunciation, is always passionate; for all his likes are intense, and his hates are equally strong. His contempt for the men and things he despises is refreshing in these days of lukewarm and well-regulated emotions. I think the very most lovable thing about him is his absolute frankness. With those whom he regards as friends he is as open as a child, and as ready to reveal his real self—a self fuller of sweetness and justice and generosity than any one will ever guess who judges him from his somewhat fiery newspaper controversies, or the comments of superficial observers.

The most distinguished, or at least the best known, of Swinburne's poetical disciples, is Oscar Wilde, who has won his fame, however, more as a social leader of the new æsthetic movement than as a poet. Some anecdotes illustrating the prominent characteristics of this gentleman are given in the subjoined letter to the *Boston Herald*.

### AN ENGLISH ÆSTHETE.

The poet Wilde's dream of fair women began with Mrs. Langtry and ended with Mme. Modjeska, whom he worshipped with a certain chaste devotion infinitely touching, for, although he was "always" at the Polish star's receptions and first representations, she treated him only with the same politeness and amiability which she is accustomed to extend to every one who is a habitué of her drawing-room. As for Mrs. Langtry, I believe that she viewed him in the light of a wild lunatic; when his rhapsodies and dreams failed to amuse her, she was seen less frequently at his rose-colored afternoon teas, one peculiarity of which was that the light was kept so dim in twilight atmosphere, accelerated by drawn blinds, that few people were able to recognize anybody they encountered there. Mrs. Langtry, sometimes the bright, particular star of these mysterious gatherings, allowed, while there on one occasion, an American journalist of engaging frankness to be introduced to her. "Well, Mrs. Langtry," he said, "I'm glad to have a look at you for myself, and I am also happy to say that, in my humble opinion, you are all that you've been represented." The Jersey Lily smiled graciously and bowed her thanks for this "knock-down" compliment. Fortunately Oscar did not overhear it. Some time after our poet Wilde answered in an inquiry as to which of two ladies was Mrs. Langtry, with a curl of the lip and the following outburst: "What an absurd question! If the sun shone I should know it were the sun!" Sandwiched between "the sun that shone" and "the haunting eyes" of the gifted Modjeska was Mlle. Sarah Bernhardt, at whose house in Prince's Gate Oscar established himself on a somewhat friendly footing as one of countless admirers. He converses sufficiently well in French to be able to carry on elaborate discussions with the then reigning favorite, but Sarah was not well enough posted as regards his precise status in the artistic world to understand exactly how to estimate these enunciations, and her ideas about him and his works are of the vaguest possible description, or were at last accounts. If she were asked who he was she would be puzzled to answer, though she might safely describe him as "a great poet—a sort of Lord Byron and *eau sucrée*." Oscar has a mania for distinguished foreigners. He was present at some of the sittings which Mr. Henry Irving gave to Bastien Lepage, the painter, and acted, indeed, as interpreter between the gifted Gaul and the tragedian, who does not speak French, but is content, in the language of Hon. Bardwell Slote, "to wrestle with the vernacular." As an instance of Bastien Lepage's eye for detail, Oscar related the following anecdote: "I will paint in your glass of milk," said the Frenchman. "How did you know I drank milk?" responded the tragedian. "Oh," was Bastien Lepage's reply, "I noticed an empty glass, that had had milk in, on a tray as I came up stairs." Oscar was quite content to translate at this interesting series of interviews. He admires the great tragedian, and is the author of the now well-known line, "Don't you think that Irving's left leg is very expressive?" and, perhaps, even of the reply, "Yes, and his left leg is so much more expressive than the right!" Oscar is, however, impartial in his admiration of artists; he has an eye for "the beautiful" in whatever mould; and much more dignified than the note recently published, as having been addressed to Miss Genevieve Ward, were the lines he penned to Mr. John McCullough, after witnessing his debut at "Old Drury," as *Virginius*. "It is long," he said, "since we have had here in England such a noble representative of the antique world."

Although the poet Wilde has been accused of himself deliberately supplying Du Maurier with material for the Maudle and Postlethwaite cuts in *Punch*, including the "Let us try to live up to it" tea-pot, and the drawing, supplemented by the statement that he never bathed, because he disliked to see himself foreshortened in the water, it is almost certain that he really objected to Mr. Beerbohm Tree's singularly accurate reproduction of him in the comedy of "Where's the Cat?" at the Criterion theatre. Beerbohm Tree had studied Oscar's peculiarities very closely, and his caricature—if it can be called such—was instantly recognized by press and public. I was present the night when "one of the two beauties," Lady Lonsdale, came to see this play, and the name "Oscar Wilde!" passed from lip to lip the moment the clever Beerbohm Tree set foot upon the stage, one trouser-leg turned up at the bottom, after the manner of our poet, who did not rest until he had written the actor an indignant letter, in which he protested against his having taken advantage of "the accident" of their acquaintance. Mr. Beerbohm Tree, whose brother, by the way, is the author of the verses styled " The Æsthetic Maiden's Lament," thereupon replied that he had reproduced not an individual, but a type. About this time Oscar appeared in counterfeit presentment in the shop windows, arrayed in velvet garb, a Byronic collar, and his wonted placid smile. He also adopted a new article of attire, a furred overcoat, which he was known to wear heroically throughout receptions in hot rooms where every one else was stifling. Oscar was brave enough to attend the first performance of " The Colonel," although he had been warned that " the æsthetic craze " was to be travestied ; he sat through the piece in solemn silence, very much disgusted at the bad taste of the Philistines, to whom nothing is sacred ; but it is a question whether the people around him got more enjoyment out of the sport of the stage, or the drooping attitude of the only Oscar. " Patience " completed the work of theatrical devastation, and the ridicule of the stage has absolutely frightened many æsthetes into everyday garb, albeit not into commonplace conversation. The undaunted Wilde was, last summer, however, at a supper party graced by the presence of the Prince of Wales, Mr. Arthur Sullivan, and Mr. George Grossmith, at which the comedian just named consented to sing Budthorne's solo. The presence of the original of the " Pure young man " gave additional zest to the inimitable verses, and, at their close, the admirer of "a bashful young potato or a not too French French bean" was dragged bodily up before H. R. H., with the words: "This is the man." Oscar's countenance, despite royalty's gracious consideration, expressed intense disgust. About this time, look out for "squalls!" Derby day the announcement of forthcoming poems blossomed in placards on every bush and tree—literally, every stone wall in London-town; they came in white and gold, and you know how they were received—better here than in England. Apart from the fact that a prophet is not without honor save in his own country, there seemed to be an impression on this side, that Oscar Wilde was an out-and-out idiot, whereas it was known in England that he was only pretending to be one. His poem on "England," clever, if too Tennysonian, appeared originally in Edmund Yates' paper, the *World*, and was duly parodied in *Truth*. For a long time Mr. Labouchere ignored Oscar almost altogether, but he has lately espoused his side in a gratuitous insult put upon him by a college librarian who returned the volume of poems which Mr. Wilde had sent in response to a request. It was rumored at one time that Oscar would appear as an actor, but this probably had its foundation in the fact that he has at least written a play, the "Vera," which has yet to see the garish lamps, but may be done in this country.

One of the most scathing reviews, which appeared anent the white-and-gold poems, was printed in *Vanity Fair*, for which publication Mr. Willie Wilde, brother of the aforesaid Oscar, writes theatrical criticisms. In this instance a journalistic Cain did not slay a poetic Abel. It was a stranger—or, at all events, not Willie—a young gentleman who has managed to assert himself, despite the supremacy of his more conspicuous relative. If ever Oscar wants to write as "Don Juan," here is the model in his own family. William is dark and well-looking, inclined to corpulency, and, alas! belongs to the Lotus Club, Regent Street. Both men are good sons. The "Speranza" of Irish poetry is the pseudonym that hides the personality of Lady Wilde, whom mortal eyes of late years have not seen without at least one vail, and perhaps two. Lady Wilde is tall and ample in figure, and still clings to the crinoline; in voluminous silken robes of black and crimson she moves about, balloon-like, as though impelled by some unknown agency. This accomplished gentleman does not go much into society—not so much, that is to say, as Oscar, who cannot be a great deal at his present residence, Keats House, Tite Street, Chelsea, the combined house and studio of his *alter ego*, Frank Miles, the artist.

# CHAPTER XIV.

## THE BROWNINGS.

Reminiscences of Miss Mitford and Miss Martineau—A day with the Brownings at Pratolino—Hawthorne's two meetings with the poet and his wife.

IN May, 1836, Miss Mary Russell Mitford, writing home from London to her father about a visit she had made to the "giraffes and the Diorama," tells him that "a sweet young woman, whom we called for in Gloucester Place, went with us—a Miss Barrett—who reads Greek as I do French, and has published some translations from Æschylus, and some most striking poems. She is a delightful young creature, shy and timid, and modest. Nothing but desire to see me got her out at all. * * * She is so sweet and gentle, and so pretty, that one looks at her as if she were some bright flower; and she says that it is like a dream that she should be talking to me whose works she knows by heart." Miss Barrett was then twenty-seven; but she had so youthful a look that Miss Mitford found it difficult to persuade a friend that this translatess of the "Prometheus," the authoress of the "Essay on Mind," was old enough to be introduced into company!

In the "Autobiography" of another literary lady we get a glimpse of the future husband of Miss Barrett, as he appeared about the time Miss Mitford writes of.

A poet whose face I was always glad to see, [Harriet Martineau says], was Browning. It was in the days when he had not yet seen the Barretts. I did not know them either. When I was ill at Tynemouth, a correspondence grew up between the then bedridden Elizabeth Barrett and myself; and a very intimate correspondence it became. In one of the later letters, in telling me how much better she was, and how grievously disappointed at being prevented going to Italy, she wrote of going out, of basking in the open sunshine, of doing this and that; "in short," said she, finally, "there is no saying what foolish thing I may do." The "foolish thing" evidently in view in this passage was marrying Robert Browning; and a truly wise act did the foolish thing turn out to be. I had never seen my correspondent, for she had gone to Italy before I left Tynemouth; but I knew her husband well, about twenty years ago. It was a wonderful event to me—my first acquaintance with his poetry. Mr. Macready put "Paracelsus" into my hands, when I was staying at his house; and I read a canto before going to bed. For the first time in my life, I passed a whole night without sleeping a wink. The unbounded expectation I formed from that poem was sadly disappointed when "Sordello" came out. I was so wholly unable to understand it that I supposed myself ill. But in conversation no speaker could be more absolutely clear and purpose-like. He was full of good sense and fine feeling, amidst occasional irritability; full also of fun and harmless satire; with some little affectations which were as droll as any thing he said. A real genius was Robert Browning, assuredly; and how good a man, how wise and morally strong, is proved by the successful issue of the perilous experiment of the marriage of two poets. They are a remarkable pair, whom society may well honor and cherish.

The story of the marriage of these poets has been told in many ways, and the following article, written for *Scribner's Monthly*, by Mrs. Elizabeth C. Kinney, and relating the tale as it fell from Mr. Browning's own lips, is consequently of much interest.

A DAY WITH THE BROWNINGS AT PRATOLINO.

It was my privilege to live for years near by, and in intimate intercourse with, the divinity of Casa Guidi,

—her whose genius has immortalized the walls as well as the windows of that antique palace ; for a tablet has been inserted by the grateful Italians, whose cause she so eloquently espoused, in the grand entrance wall, recording her name, deeds, and long residence there, with the tribute of their thanks and love. Yet I had not known the Brownings personally, in the more intimate sense of acquaintanceship, till that blessed day, when, in the balm of a June morning, we started together in an open carriage for Pratolino, taking with us a man-servant, who carried the basket containing our picnic dinner, of which only four were to partake. A larger party would have spoiled the whole. A more timid nature was never joined to a bolder spirit than in Elizabeth Browning. She fairly shrunk from observation, and could not endure mixed company, though in her heart kind and sympathetic with all. Her timidity was both instinctive and acquired ; having been an invalid and student from her youth up, she had lived almost the life of a recluse ; thus it shocked her to be brought face to face with inquisitive strangers, or the world in general. On this very account, and because her health so rarely permitted her to make excursions of any kind, she enjoyed, as the accustomed do not, and the unappreciative cannot, any unwonted liberty in nature's realm, and doubly with a chosen few sympathetic companions, to whom she could freely express her thoughts and emotions. Like most finely-strung beings, she spoke through a changeful countenance every change of feeling.

Never shall I forget how her face—the plain mortal beautiful in its immortal expression—lighted up to greet us as our carriage drove into the *porte-cochère* of Casa Guidi on that memorable morning. Simple as a child, the honest enjoyment which she anticipated in our excursion beamed through her countenance. Those large, dark, dreamy eyes—usually like deep wells of thought—sparkled with delight; while her adored Robert's generous capacity for pleasure showed even a happier front than ordinary, reflecting her joy, as we turned into the street and out at the city gate toward Pratolino. The woman of usually many thoughts and few words grew a talker under the stimulus of open country air; while her husband, usually talkative, became the silent enjoyer of her vocal gladness, a pleasure too rarely afforded him to be interrupted. We, of choice, only talked enough to keep our *improvvisatrice* in the humor of utterance. Every tree, every wayside flower, every uncommon stone or passing cloud, gave fresh impulse to her spirit, which verily seemed like an enfranchised bird's. On reaching the enchanting grounds of Pratolino—which royal love enchanted as long ago as the sixteenth century—we all began to talk of the past, till the present was animated by its spirit; breathing beauty seemed stirring the leaves of green retreats, made for love; inspiring the songs of numerous birds, whose musical *amours* enjoy now unmolested those right royal groves; vitalizing the gold and silver fishes which sport in those silver lakes, all unconscious of the rapturous faces once mirrored there. Even the climbing roses encircled those ancient walls with beauty, and conjured fragrant memories of a dead yet living past. As we neared the villa, no wonder that poetic fancy seized that enthusiastic group, and we saw the beautiful Bianca strolling among the flowers with her infatuated lover, herself not more fond than ambitious to share his ducal crown. The very insects seemed whispering of that tragic romance, and our queen of song relapsed into dreams which we dared not disturb, till, threading our path silently along the winding ways, we at length entered a grove in the rear of the villa, where, with one accord, we paused for rest and refreshment. By this time the reaction of languor after unwonted excitement came over Mrs. Browning; she almost fell prostrate on the grass, where she lay with closed eyes, a stone for her pillow, like Jacob in his dream,—and doubtless she also had a vision of the ladder on which the angels were descending and ascending, as her ministers.

Withdrawing a short distance, so that our mellowed voices might not reach her, while lunch was being prepared under the trees, Robert Browning put on his talking-cap again, and discoursed, to two delighted listeners, of her who slept. After expressing his joy at her enjoyment of the morning, the poet's soul took fire by its own friction, and glowed with the brilliance of its theme. Knowing well that he was before fervent admirers of his wife, he did not fear to speak of her genius, which he did almost with awe, losing himself so entirely in her glory that one could see that he did not feel worthy to unloose her shoe-latchet, much less to call her his own. This led back to the birth of his first love for her, and then, without reserve, he told us the real story of that romance, "the course of" which "true love never did run smooth." There have been several printed stories of the loves of Elizabeth and Robert Browning, and we had read some of these; but as the poet's own tale differed essentially from the others, and as the divine genius of the heroine has returned to its native heaven, whilst her life on earth now belongs to posterity, it cannot be a breach of confidence to let the truth be known.

Mr. Barrett, the father of Elizabeth, though himself a superior man, and capable of appreciating his gifted child, was, in some sense, an eccentric. He had an unaccountable aversion to the idea of "marrying off" any of his children. Having wealth, a sumptuous house, and being a widower, he had somehow made up his mind to keep them all about him. Elizabeth, the eldest, had been an invalid from her early youth, owing partly to the great shock which her exquisite nervous organization received when she saw an idolized brother drown before her eyes, without having the power to save him. Grief at this event naturally threw her much within herself, while shattered health kept her confined for years to her room. There she thought, studied, wrote; and from her sick-chamber went forth the winged inspirations of her genius. These came into the heart of Robert Browning, and, nesting there, awakened love for "The Great Unknown," and he sought her out. Finding that the invalid did not receive strangers, he wrote her a letter, intense with his desire to see her. She reluctantly consented to an interview. He flew to her apartment, was admitted by the nurse, in whose presence only could he see the deity at whose shrine he had long worshipped. But the golden opportunity was not to be lost; love became oblivious to any save the presence of the real of its ideal. Then and there Robert Browning poured his impassioned soul into hers, though his tale of love seemed only an enthusiast's dream. Infirmity had hitherto so hedged her about that she deemed herself for ever protected from all assaults of love. Indeed, she felt only injured that a fellow-poet should take advantage, as it were, of her indulgence in granting him an interview, and requested him to withdraw from her presence, not attempting any response to his proposal, which she could not believe in earnest. Of course he withdrew from her sight, but not to withdraw the offer of his heart and hand; *au contraire*, to repeat it by letter, and in such wise as to convince her how "dead in earnest" he was. Her own heart, touched already when she knew it not, was this time fain to listen, be convinced, and overcome. But here began the tug of war! As a filial daughter, Elizabeth told her father of the poet's love, of the poet's love in return, and asked a parent's blessing to crown their happiness. At first, incredulous of the strange story, he mocked her; but when the truth flashed on him, from the new fire in her eyes, he kindled with rage, and forbade her ever seeing or communicating with her lover again, on the penalty of disinheritance and banishment for ever from a father's love. This decision was founded on no dislike for Mr. Browning personally, or any thing in him, or his family; it was simply arbitrary. But the new love was stronger than the old in her—it conquered. On wings it flew to her beloved, who had perched on her window, and thence bore her away from the fogs of England to a nest under Italian skies. The nightingale who had long sung in the dark, with "her breast against a thorn," now changed into a lark—morning had come—singing for very joy, and at heaven's gate, which has since opened to let her in.

The unnatural father kept his vow, and would never be reconciled to his daughter, of whom he was not worthy; though she ceased not her endearing efforts to find her way to his heart again; ever fearing that he, or she, might die without the bond of forgiveness having reunited them. Always cherishing an undiminished love for her only parent, this banishment from him wore on her, notwithstanding the rich compensation of such a husband's devotion, and the new maternal love which their golden-haired boy awakened. What she feared, came upon her! Her father died without leaving her even his pardon, and her feeble *physique* never quite recovered from the shock. Few witnessed the strong grief of that morally strong woman. I saw her after her first wrestling with the angel of sorrow, and perceived that with the calm token of his blessing, still she dragged a maimed life.

To return to Pratolino : The poet's story of his love had sharpened appetite, and we gathered at the rustic table in the grove, where our queen, Elizabeth, crowned the feast. Recovered by rest from the morning's fatigue, she was able to join, though not again to lead, our conversation. Under the stimulus of appetizing viands, and good wine in moderation, Robert Browning's spirits overflowed, even to the confession of telling us their romance, receiving only from its heroine the slight punishment of her, " Robert, dear ! how could you ? "

After lunch we all went to the brow of the hill, and together looked out on that marvellous view, backed by the Apennines in their afternoon glory; while before us lay dreamily, under a softening mist-veil, Florence the Beautiful!—its massive palaces, with their ponderous eaves; its majestic Duomo; its heaven-pointing Campanile,—that perfection of symmetry; its arching bridges, spanning the classic Arno, which curved like a silver thread amidst all that scene of loveliness. There the past and the present met together; terror and beauty embraced each other. All that Elizabeth Browning said, after gazing awhile in silence, was, "How it speaks to us!" Since then it has spoken to us again through the echo from her spirit; we caught it even then, and though that spirit has since passed away, the echo of its own song has not died, shall not die; Elizabeth Browning "was for all time!"

We returned to Florence just as the sun was setting behind the Tuscan hills, and the moon rising on our forward path as a welcome. When we rolled under the arched gateway of Casa Guidi, a tired voice said, faintly, "How I thank you!" while in heartiest tone Robert Browning repeated, "Ay, thanks for a real pleasure-day." As for us, we could only claim our right to all the thanksgiving, and respond, "Yes, a day to be remembered, and ——" recorded here!

Hawthorne met the Brownings in England,

and again in Italy, and he has made a record of both meetings in his " Note-Books." The first occasion was at one of the famous literary breakfasts given by Richard Monckton Milnes (the present Lord Houghton), of which Hawthorne gives the following account.

### A LONDON LITERARY BREAKFAST.

*July* 13, 1856. On Friday morning (11th) I took the rail into town to breakfast with Mr. Milnes. * * * Whether I was quite beyond rule I cannot say ; but it did not lack more than ten minutes of eleven when I was ushered up stairs and I found all the company assembled. However, it is of little consequence, except that if I had come early I should have been introduced to many of the guests, whom now I could only know across the table.

Mr. Milnes introduced me to Mrs. Browning, and assigned her to me to conduct into the breakfast-room. She is a small, delicate woman, with ringlets of dark hair, a pleasant, intelligent, and sensitive face, and a low, agreeable voice. She looks youthful and comely, and is very gentle and lady-like. And so we proceeded to the breakfast-room, which is hung round with pictures ; and in the middle of it stood a large round table, worthy to have been King Arthur's, and here we seated ourselves without any question of precedence or ceremony. On one side of me was an elderly lady, with a very fine countenance, and in the course of breakfast I discovered her to be the mother of Florence Nightingale. One of her daughters (not Florence) was likewise present. Mrs. Milnes, Mrs. Browning, Mrs. Nightingale, and her daughter were the only ladies at table; and I think there were as many as eight or ten gentlemen, whose names—as I came so late—I was left to find out for myself, or to leave unknown. Mrs. Browning and I talked a great deal during breakfast, for she is of that quickly appreciative and responsive order of women with whom I can talk more freely than with any man; and she has, besides, her own originality, wherewith to help on conversation, though I should say not of a loquacious tendency. She introduced the subject of spiritualism, which, she says, interests her very much; indeed, she seems to be a believer. Mr. Browning, she told me, utterly rejects the subject, and will not believe even in the outward manifestations, of which there is such overwhelming evidence. We also talked of Miss Bacon, and I developed something of that lady's theories respecting Shakespeare, greatly to the horror of Mrs. Browning and that of her next neighbor,—a nobleman whose name I did not hear. On the whole, I like her the better for loving the man Shakespeare with a personal love. We spoke, too, of Margaret Fuller, who spent her last night in Italy with the Brownings; and of William Story, with whom they have been intimate, and who, Mrs. Browning says, is much stirred about Spiritualism. Really, I cannot help wondering that so fine a spirit as hers should not reject the matter till, at least, it is forced upon her. I like her very much.

Mrs. Nightingale had been talking at first with Lord Lansdowne, who sat next her, but by and by she turned to me and began to speak of London smoke. Then, there being a discussion about Lord Byron on the other side of the table, she spoke to me about Lady Byron, whom she knows intimately, characterizing her as a most excellent and exemplary person, high-principled, unselfish, and now devoting herself to the care of her two grandchildren,—their mother, Byron's daughter, being dead. Lady Byron, she says, writes beautiful verses. Somehow or other, all this praise, and more of the same kind, gave us an idea of an intolerably irreproachable person; and I asked Mrs. Nightingale if Lady Byron were warm-hearted. With some hesitation, or mental reservation,—at all events, not quite outspokenly,—she answered that she was.

I was too much engaged with these personal talks to attend much to what was going on elsewhere; but all through breakfast I had been more and more impressed by the aspect of one of the guests, sitting next to Milnes. He was a man of large presence, a portly personage, gray-haired, but scarcely as yet aged; and his face had a remarkable intelligence, not vivid nor sparkling, but conjoined with great quietude,—and if it gleamed or brightened at one time more than another, it was like the sheen over a broad surface of sea. There was a somewhat careless self-possession, large and broad enough to be called dignity; and the more I looked at him the more I knew that he was a distinguished person, and wondered who. He might have been a minister of state; only there is not one of them who has any right to such a face and presence. At last—I do not know how the conviction came,—but I became aware that it was Macaulay, and began to see some slight resemblance to his portraits. But I have not seen any that is not wretchedly unworthy of the original. As soon as I knew him, I began to listen to his conversation, but he did not talk a great deal—contrary to his usual custom. For I am told he is apt to engross all the talk to himself. Probably he may have been restrained by the presence of Ticknor and Mr. Palfrey, who were among his auditors and interlocutors, and as the conversation seemed to turn much on American subjects, he could not well have assumed to talk them down. I am glad to have seen him,—a face fit for a scholar, a man of the world, a cultivated intelligence. After we left the table and went into the library, Mr. Browning introduced himself to me—a younger man than I had expected to see, handsome, with brown hair.

He is very simple and agreeable in manner, gently impulsive, talking as if his heart were uppermost. He spoke of his pleasure in meeting me, and his appreciation of my books; and—which has not often happened to me—mentioned that the "Blithedale Romance" was the one he admired most. I wonder why. I hope I showed as much pleasure at his praise as he showed at mine; for I was glad to see how pleasantly it moved him.

Two years later, Hawthorne, in his "Italian Note-Books," makes the following entry in regard to

A VISIT TO THE BROWNINGS IN CASA GUIDI.

Florence, *June* 9, 1858.—We went last evening, at eight o'clock, to see the Brownings; and, after some search and inquiry, we found the Casa Guidi, which is a palace in a street not very far from our own. It being dusk, I could not see the exterior, which, if I remember, Browning has celebrated in song; at all events Mrs. Browning has called one of her poems "Casa Guidi Windows." The street is a narrow one; but on entering the palace we found a spacious staircase and ample accommodations of vestibule and hall, the latter opening on a balcony where we could hear the chanting of priests in a church close by. Browning told us that this was the first church where an oratorio had ever been performed. He came into the anteroom to greet us, as did his little boy, Robert, whom they call Pennini for fondness. The latter cognomen is a diminutive of Apennino, which was bestowed upon him at his first advent into the world because he was so very small, there being a statue in Florence of colossal size called Apennino. I never saw such a boy as this before; so slender, fragile, and spirit-like,—not as if he were actually in ill health, but as if he had little or nothing to do with human flesh and blood. His face is very pretty and most intelligent, and exceedingly like his mother's. He is nine years old, and seems at once less childlike and less manly than would befit that age. I should not quite like to be the father of such a boy, and should fear to stake so much interest and affection on him as he cannot fail to inspire.

Mrs. Browning met us at the door of the drawing-room and greeted us most kindly,—a pale, small person, scarcely embodied at all; at any rate only substantial enough to put forth her slender fingers to be grasped, and to speak with a shrill yet sweet tenuity of voice. Really, I do not see how Mr. Browning can suppose that he has an earthly wife any more than an earthly child; both are of the elfin race, and will flit away from him some day when he least thinks of it. She is a good and kind fairy, however, and sweetly disposed toward the human race, although only remotely akin to it. It is wonderful to see how small she is, how pale her cheek, how bright and dark her eyes. There is not such another figure in the world, and black ringlets cluster down her neck and make her face look the whiter by their sable profusion. I could not form any judgment about her age; it may range anywhere within the limits of human life or elfin life. When I met her in London at Lord Houghton's breakfast-table she did not impress me so singularly; for the morning light is more prosaic than the dim illumination of their great tapestried drawing-room; and, besides, sitting next to her she did not have occasion to raise her voice in speaking, and I was not sensible what a slender voice she has. It is marvellous to me how so extraordinary, so acute, so sensitive a creature can impress us, as she does, with the certainty of her benevolence. It seems to me there were a million chances to one that she would have been a miracle of acidity and bitterness.

We were not the only guests. Mr. and Mrs. E——, Americans, recently from the East, and on intimate terms with the Brownings, arrived after us; also Miss F. H——, an English literary lady whom I have met several times in Liverpool; and lastly came the white head and palmer-like beard of Mr. —— [Bryant] with his daughter. Mr. Browning was very efficient in keeping up conversation with everybody, and seemed to be in all parts of the room and in every group at the same moment, a most vivid and quick-thoughted person, logical and common-sensible, as, I presume, poets generally are in their daily talk. Mr. —— as usual was homely and plain of manner, with an old-fashioned dignity, nevertheless, and a remarkable deference and gentleness of tone in addressing Mrs. Browning. I doubt, however, whether he has any high appreciation either of her poetry or her husband's, and it is my impression that they care as little about his.

We had some tea and some strawberries, and passed a pleasant evening. There was no very noteworthy conversation: the most interesting topic being that disagreeable and now wearisome one of spiritual communications, as regards which Mrs. Browning is a believer and her husband an infidel. Mr.—— appeared not to have made up his mind on the matter, but told a story of a successful communication between Cooper the novelist and his sister, who had been dead fifty years. Browning and his wife had both been present at a spiritual session held by Mr. Hume, and had seen and felt the unearthly hands, one of which had placed a laurel wreath on Mrs. Browning's head. Browning, however, avowed a belief that these hands were affixed to the feet of Mr. Hume, who lay extended in his chair, with his legs stretched far under the table. The marvellousness of the fact, as I have read it, and heard it from other eye-witnesses, melted strangely away in his hearty gripe and at the sharp touch of his logic ; while his wife, ever and anon, put in a little gentle word of expostulation.

I am rather surprised that Browning's conversation should be so clear, and so much to the purpose at the moment, since his poetry can seldom proceed far without running into the high grass of latent meanings and obscure allusions.

Later on Hawthorne speaks of meeting Mr. Browning at Mrs. Trollope's house, where he was "very genial and full of life, as usual, but his conversation had the effervescent aroma which you cannot catch, even if you get the very words that seem to be imbued with it. Browning's nonsense is of a very genuine and excellent quality, the true bubble and effervescence of a bright and powerful mind; and he lets it play among his friends with the faith and simplicity of a child. He must be an amiable man. I should like him much, and should make him like me, if opportunities were favorable."

## CHAPTER XV.

### CHARLES DICKENS.

*Blanchard Jerrold's reminiscences—A woman's gossip—The Dickens banquet described by an eye-witness.*

IT is generally agreed that Dickens has suffered in popular esteem by the publication of Forster's Life. I do not very clearly see why. The impression which Mr. Forster gives of his hero is that of a bluff and hearty egotist, whose respect for his own abilities was as unmeasured as it was sincere, and whose fondness for the striking and the melodramatic sometimes allowed him to degenerate into vulgarity. But it needed no great keenness of vision to read these qualities between the lines of his books, and in any event they are minor defects; they need not blind us to what was manly and generous and admirable in his character. His very egotism had no smallness or meanness about it—perhaps because it was so thoroughgoing. It was the egotism of a man who was too sure of himself to have any fear of rivalry, and who could afford to be generous. Moreover, it was his natural disposition to be generous. "Those who knew him best and closest," says Blanchard Jerrold, "saw how little he would ever produce to the outer world of the bright, chivalrous, engaging, and deep and tender heart that beat within his bosom. The well of kindness was open to mankind, and from it generations will drink; but it was never fathomed." And Mr. Jerrold goes on to give the following

### REMINISCENCES OF DICKENS.

Charles Dickens, as all writers about him have testified, was so graciously as well as lavishly endowed by Nature, that every utterance was sunny, every sentiment pure, every emotional opinion instinctively right,—like a woman's. The head that governed the richly-stored heart was wise, prompt, and alert at the same time. He communicated to all he did the delightful sense of ease with power. The air about him vibrated with his activity, and his surprising vitality. In a difficulty men felt safe merely because he was present. Most easily, among all thinkers it has been my fortune to know, was he master of every situation in which he placed himself. Not only because of the latent, conscious power that was in him, and the knightly cheerfulness which became the pure-minded servant of humanity who had used himself to victory; but because he adopted always the old plain advice, and deliberated well before he acted with the vigor which was inseparable from any activity of his.

The art with which Charles Dickens managed men and women was nearly all emotional. As in his books he drew at will upon the tears of his readers, in his life he helped men with a spontaneous grace and sweetness which are indescribable. The deep, rich, cheery voice; the brave and noble countenance; the hand that had the fire of friendship in its grip,—all played their part in comforting in a moment the creature who had come to Charles Dickens for advice, for help, for sympathy. When he took a cause in hand, or a friend under his wing, people who knew him breathed in a placid sense of security. He had not only the cordial will to be of use wherever his services could be advantageously enlisted, but he could see at a glance the exact thing he might do; and beyond the range of his conviction as to his own power, or the limit of proper asking or advancing, no power on earth could move him the breadth of a hair.

When Ada, Lady Lovelace, was dying, and suffering the tortures of a slow, internal disease, she expressed a craving to see Charles Dickens, and talk with him. He went to her, and found a mourning house. The lady was stretched upon a couch, heroically enduring her agony. The appearance of Dickens' earnest, sympathetic face was immediate relief. She asked him whether the attendant had left a basin of ice and a spoon. *She had.* "Then give me some now and then, and don't notice me when I crush it between my teeth : it soothes my pain, and—we can talk."

The womanly tenderness, the wholeness with which Dickens would enter into the delicacies of such a situation, will rise instantly to the mind of all who knew him. That he was at the same moment the most careful of nurses and the most sympathetic and sustaining of comforters, who can doubt?

"Do you ever pray?" the poor lady asked.

"Every morning and every evening," was Dickens' answer, in that rich, sonorous voice which crowds happily can remember ; but of which they can best understand all the eloquence, who knew how simple and devout he was when he spoke of sacred things, —of suffering, of wrong, or of misfortune. "He taught the world," said his friend Dean Stanley over his new-made grave in Westminster Abbey, " great lessons of the eternal value of generosity, of purity, of kindness, and of unselfishness ; and by his fruits shall he be known of all men." His engaging manner when he came suddenly in contact with a sick friend, defies description ; but from his own narrative of his walk with my father, which he told me made his heart heavy and was a gloomy task, it is easy for friends to understand the patience, solicitude, kindly counsel, and designed humor with which he went through with it. My father was very ill; but under Dickens' thoughtful care he had rallied before they had reached the Temple. "We strolled through the Temple," Dickens wrote me, "on our way to a boat, and I have a lively recollection of him stamping about Elm Tree Court, with his hat in one hand, and the other pushing his hair back, laughing in his heartiest manner at a ridiculous remembrance we had in common, which I had presented in some exaggerated light to divert him." Then again, of the same day: "The dinner-party was a large one, and I did not sit near him at table. But he and I arranged, before we went in to dinner, that he was only to eat some simple dish that we agreed upon, and was only to drink sherry-and-water." Then, "We exchanged, 'God bless you!' and shook hands."

And—they never met again.

But how full of wise consideration is all this day spent with the invalid friend, in the midst of merriment, even to the ridiculous remembrance "presented in some exaggerated light, to divert him!" Mr. Charles Kent has told me how he met Dickens a few weeks before his death, and was observed, at a glance, by that most masterly and piercing observer, to be in low spirits and feeble. Whereupon Dickens, who had ample momentous business of his own on hand, put it aside, sketched a pleasant day together: a *tête-à-tête* dinner and a walk. In short, to watch the many sides of his unselfishness, and the fund of resources for the good of other people he had at his command, was to be astonished at his extraordinary vitality. How good he was to all who had the slightest claim on him, who shall tell? But that which Hepworth Dixon said over my father's dust may be assuredly repeated by the narrow bed near Macaulay, Sheridan, and Handel. If every one who has received a favor at the hands of Dickens should cast a flower upon his grave, a mountain of roses would lie upon the great man's breast. And, in truth, his grave was filled with flowers.

There was that boy-element in Charles Dickens which has been so often remarked in men of genius as to appear almost inseparable from the highest gifts of nature. "Why, we played a game of knock 'em down only a week or two ago," a friend remarked to me last June, with brimming eyes. "And he showed all the old, astonishing energy and delight in taking aim at Aunt Sally."

My own earliest recollections of Charles Dickens are of his gayest moods: when the boy in him was exuberant, and leap-frog or rounders were not sports too young for the player who had written "Pickwick" twenty years before. To watch him through an afternoon, by turns light and grave; gracious and loving and familiar to the young, apt and vigorous in council with the old; ready for a frolic upon the lawn—leap-frog, rounders; as ready for a committee-meeting in the library; and then to catch his cheery good-night, and feel the hand that spoke so truly from the heart,—was to see Charles Dickens the man, the friend, the companion, and the counsellor, all at once, and to get at something like a just estimate of that which was beautiful in the brilliant and noble Englishman we have lost.

The following interesting chapter of gossip, contributed originally to the *Englishwoman's Magazine*, gives us perhaps the most vivid and striking portraiture of Dickens the man, that is to be found in any sketch of similar length.

### A WOMAN'S GOSSIP.

Even the trivialities connected with a great man are interesting, and the *mildest* anecdotes of a hero's private life are full of flavor to those who know him only on the pedestal of his public career. It is not my intention to enter into any of the vexed questions regarding his domestic unhappiness, but to merely give a true detail of my impressions of him during the period of the few months in which I was in daily intercourse with Charles Dickens and his family. These reminiscences of him, though disinterred from the memories of nearly twenty-nine years ago, may still afford amusement to others, as they do to me in recalling them. So vivid is my first impression of our great author that I can see him now "in my mind's eye" as clearly depicted as if days, and not years, had intervened since I was presented to him at the house of a relative of mine. I was first introduced to his wife in the sanctuary of the bedroom, where I was arranging my hair before the glass. I thought her a pretty little woman, with the heavy-lidded large blue eyes so much admired by men. The nose was a little *retroussé*, the forehead good, mouth small, round, and red-lipped, with a pleasant smiling expression, notwithstanding the sleepy look of the slow-moving eyes. The weakest part of the face was the chin, which melted too suddenly into the throat. She took kindly notice of me, and I went down with a fluttering heart to be introduced to "Boz."

The *first* ideas that flashed through me were, "What a fine characteristic face! What *marvellous* eyes! And what horrid taste in dress!"

He wore his hair long, in "admired disorder," and it suited the picturesque style of his head; but he had on a surtout with a very wide collar, very much thrown back, showing a vast expanse of waistcoat, drab trousers, and drab boots with patent leather toes, and the whole effect (apart from his fine head) gave evidence of a *loud* taste in costume, and was not proper for evening dress.

Of course, I listened eagerly during dinner to catch the pearls and other precious things that fell from his lips, and watched, in reverent admiration, every flash of his clear gray eyes, for I was enthusiastic, and in my teens. He did not speak much, and his utterance was low-toned and rapid, with a certain thickness, as if the tongue were too large for the mouth. I found afterward that this was a family characteristic; and he had a habit of sucking his tongue when thinking, and at the same time running his fingers through his hair till it stood out in most leonine fashion. When writing, if his ideas got entangled, he would work away with his left hand, dragging viciously at certain locks until the subject became satisfactorily "evolved out of his inner consciousness."

Before uttering an amusing speech I noticed a most humorous scintillation gleaming in his eyes, accompanied by a comic elevation of one eyebrow; but he did not strike me as possessing the sarcastic, searching expression that I expected. I discovered afterward, that without appearing to notice what was going on around, nothing escaped him; and at the times when his eyes had a far-off look, wide-opened and almost stony in their fixity, he was in reality making mental notes of his surroundings.

How many times have I been betrayed into committing myself in thoughtless discourse, duped by his abstracted air! How often have I indulged in sundry foolish acts, and given utterance to much silly *persiflage* and ill-digested reasoning among our circle, in the full confidence of his being in the seventh heaven of rapt reverie, to find him suddenly rising up, shaking his mane like a lion from his slumbers, and, with a face radiant with mischief and fun, recapitulating all my girlish "slip-slop," twisting and turning it into the most unexpectedly distorted shapes, and tacking on to it a running commentary of witty criticisms!

He never thought himself too great a genius to enter into our games, but he somehow always contrived to transfuse such a tone of cleverness and depth into them that they became "keen encounters of our wits," and we were all put on our mettle to play *up* to the subtile spirit with which the mastermind impregnated the most sterile matter. How proud I used to feel whenever I had said a better thing than usual to get an approving smile or word from our *maestro!* The first time he thus noticed me is marked with a white stone in my memory. A number of us were playing the simple game of "How, when, and where do you like it?" The word given was "scull," and the object is to puzzle the querist by the several meanings given to the word. Frederick Dickens was the questioner, and I gave, in reply to "How I liked it?" "With the accompaniment of a fine organ." 2d. "When?" "When youth is at the helm and pleasure at the prow." 3d. "Where?" "Where wanders the hoary Thames along his silver winding way."

Dickens rose and came over to me, saying, laughingly, "Of course, little goose, your answers betrayed the word to the most simple comprehension, but they were good answers and apt quotations nevertheless, and I think it would add to the interest of the game if we all sharpened our wits, and tried to give a poetical tone to it by good quotations as answers." After this time we had to read up to keep pace with the fund of quaint sayings he introduced into this pastime.

Another game was nothing but a series of leading questions, which we called "Animal, mineral, or vegetable." The first time we played it, Mr. Dickens was obliged to give up, after exhausting himself in questioning. He had arrived at the facts that the article in question was vegetable, mentioned in mythological history, and belonging to a queen, and that the destiny was pathetic. After a display of his classic lore in attaining this much he gave it up, and was good-naturedly indignant at finding the subject over which he had wasted so much time and erudition was one of the tarts mentioned in the rhymes—

> "The Queen of Hearts she made some tarts,
>   Upon a summer's day;
> The Knave of Hearts he stole the tarts,
>   And took them *quite* away."

We promised in future to abstain from such unworthy subjects; but on another occasion he pulled my hair in pretended wrath, because I puzzled him with "The wax with which Ulysses stuffed the ears of his crew to prevent them hearing the songs of the sirens."

Sometimes we played vingt-et-un, and he was as playfully eager, as full of noisy glee, as the veriest school-boy. One evening his friend Mr. M—— made his appearance in a preposterously long stock which he evidently thought was perfectly *chic*. Dickens eyed it for some time with a perplexed and thoughtful demeanor.

"Halloo, Charley!" said Mr. M., "what are you staring at my stock for?"

Dickens threw into his countenance an exaggerated expression of relief from a harassing doubt, and cried

"Stock? Oh, I'm glad to know it is meant for a stock; it was so painful to think you might have intended it for a waistcoat."

A great deal of amusement was excited by Mrs. Charles Dickens perpetrating the most absurd puns, which she did with a charming expression of innocence and deprecation of her husband's wrath; while he tore his hair and writhed as if convulsed with agony. He used to pretend to be utterly disgusted, although he could neither resist laughter at the puns nor at the pretty comic *moue* she made (with eyes turned up till little of the whites was visible) after launching forth one of these absurdities.

Every autumn it was Mr. Dickens' custom to take his family to Broadstairs, and shortly after I became acquainted with him the usual flitting took place. He begged my friends Mr. and Mrs. S—— to take a house there also. This they agreed to, and I accompanied them as a visitor, to my intense delight, for I hoped to be privileged to daily enjoyment of the presence of this man of genius. And now began a time which I look back to as almost the brightest in my life, as far as enjoyment went. Every day was spent by our family and the Dickenses together, either doing the usual seaside recreations, or at each other's houses. In the familiarity which such friendly association engenders we got up ridiculous relations to each other. He pretended to be engaged in a semi-sentimental, semi-jocular, and wholly nonsensical flirtation with me as well as with Milly T——, one of my friends, a charming woman of a certain age, and we on our side acted mutual jealousy toward each other, and Mrs. Charles Dickens entered into the fun with great gusto and good-humor. My friend Milly he called his "charmer," "the beloved of his soul," and I was his "fair enslaver" and his "queen." We generally addressed each other in the old English style of euphuism, and he would ask us to dance in such bombastic nonsense as :

"Wilt tread a measure with me, sweet lady? Fain would I thread the mazes of this saraband with thee."

"Ay, fair sir, that I will right gladly; in good sooth I'll never say thee nay."

I need not say that the stately and courtly gravity with which we "trod our measure" was truly edifying, and the spectators were convulsed at the wonderful "Turveydrop" deportment of Mr. Dickens, and the Malvolio-like conceit he contrived to call into his countenance.

"I think I could act a pompous ass to perfection!" he exclaimed after one of these dances. "Let us get up some charades, and test our histrionic powers."

After some discussion, we fixed on the word "Pompadour," and he took the part of Louis XIV. Milly was a Comtesse de Soubise, and I as Madame Pompadour was supposed to be jealous of her with good cause. The first syllable represented the stiff etiquette and tiresome observances of the court of the Grand Monarque, and was acted entirely in pantomimic action. The second syllable (converted into *adore*) was a love-scene, in which Louis did a deal of inflated bombast in the ancient French style of love-making to the rival comtesse. The whole was completed by the wily mistress obtaining by stratagem a *lettre-de-cachet* from the king and consigning the rival to the Bastile, while the triumph of Pompadour was complete. This was all acted on the spur of the moment, without any costume but such drapery and finery as could be obtained readily and twisted into use. Mr. Dickens was very grandiose, although he figured in a lady's broad-brimmed hat pinned up on one side, and a rather draggled feather stuck nearly on end, which would keep turning round the wrong way.

About this time there was a rumor flying about that Dickens had gone insane, at which he was much annoyed. We were all walking on the beach one day, accompanied by a gentleman, a Mr. F——, a sculptor, who had only come down on a visit to Mr. Dickens the day before. This gentleman was, to use the mildest term, very eccentric, and did the most unaccountable things in moments of impulse. He was several yards in front of us, and was behaving in a very flighty manner. Some strangers passed him, and as they neared us stood to look after him. "Ah," said one, with a lugubrious look and a Lord-Burleigh shake of the head, "you see it's quite true! Poor Boz! What a pity to see such a wreck!" Dickens scowled at them, and then called out, "Halloo, F——, I wish you'd moderate your insane gambolings! There are fools among the British public who might mistake you for me."

These representatives of the British public slunk away, followed by the glowing anger of Dickens' eyes, which seemed to shrivel them into nothingness. Dickens walked on with inflated nostrils and compressed lips for a few moments, and then burst out laughing. "I am afraid I was rather down on those poor beggars," said he, "but I don't like that ambling ass to be taken for me."

Next day he was sitting with us, when Mr. M—— ran in with consternation in every feature, calling out, "Charley! for God's sake come and put a stop to this! There's F—— has walked out of the sea, without a rag on him, right among the people on the beach. You never saw such a scatter in your life!"

Dickens jammed his hat on his head with a muttered "D——d fool!" and tore down stairs with M——; he came back in about half an hour, and Mr. S—— asked him jokingly how he had disposed of the naked truth.

"I never dreamt in childhood's hour," said Dickens, commencing poetically and then sinking suddenly into prose, " that I should ever turn myself into a perambulating screen; but the magnanimous way in which I have sacrificed my self-esteem in bobbing and sidling about with my coat-tails spread out to shield this rampant Achilles from the chaste eyes of the fair *sect* and the innocent babbies, deserves the thanks of the nation! I told him *that* was not the place for '*poses plastiques*'; but he was so enthusiastically intent on doing the antique that I could only frantically, and I may say heroically, interpose my devoted body between him and the spectators." This was all nonsense, as he told us afterward that he found F—— had returned into the water as fast as he got out, and he had no occasion to be a screen.

Why is it that by the sea one loses an immense deal of decency? Is it that the contemplation of the "vasty deep" enlarges and expands the ideas so much that they roam out into space and become lost in its immensity? Nobody seemed profoundly shocked at this affair, which was treated quite jocularly.

A few days after this Milly accompanied me to bathe, though she did not enter the water herself. After I had got out and was dressing, we heard a splash from the next machine, succeeded by spluttering and panting, interspersed with expletives and one or two "D——ns" at the coldness of the water. We emerged from our car, and, on crossing the plank which united a long row of machines, the first object that met our eyes was Dickens disporting in the waves within six yards of us, but with only his head and shoulders visible.

"What! my charmers?" he called out, with chattering teeth. "Behold a man who has taken a fatal plunge in the briny, and wishes himself well out of it. A crab is attempting to seize my great toe, so I'm off. Ta-ta till we meet again at Philippi." And off he went swimmingly.

Like all poetical natures, he delighted in gazing at the sea. He would remain for hours as if entranced, with a rapt, immovable, sphinx-like calm on his face, and that far-off look in his magnificent eyes, totally forgetful of every thing, and abstracted from us all. We always respected his isolation, and carefully kept aloof.

I drew a sketch of him during one of these meditative moods, and showed it to a Miss F—— who was staying with them. This young lady had testified a good deal of petty jealousy at the notice which Dickens took of me, and I have no doubt wished to make a little mischief between us, as she told him privately that evening that I had been *caricaturing* him. I was surprised to find him looking stony and stand-off when I met him again, and, greatly hurt, I went to Mrs. Charles Dickens (who was always kind and good-natured), and asked her what I had done to offend him.

"Well," she answered gently, "Charles is annoyed at your having drawn a caricature of him. Miss F—— told him she had seen a horrid caricature you had made of him."

I hastily took the sketch from between the leaves of the book I was carrying, and handed it to her without a word.

"Why, this is very like him," she cried, in pleased surprise. "This is not a caricature, but a very nice sketch. Will you give it to me? I should like

Charles to see it, and he will soon be convinced that Miss F—— was mistaken. Thank you, dear," and she kissed me kindly. "Don't let the tears come into your eyes about such nonsense; it will be all right, I promise you."

She went off with it; and the same evening I saw him again, with no cloud on his brow and as pleasant as ever.

"Mr. Dickens," I said, with tears in my voice (as the French say), "how could you think I would presume to caricature you? That odious girl put that into your head because she can't bear you to be amiable to any one but herself. Horrid, red-haired thing! I can't think why you like her!"

"My enslaver," he replied, with the odd twinkle of the eye, "I always loved gingerbread, even after childhood's hours had vanished into the dim past, and her tresses awaken fond memories of my lollipop days; but I don't like her ginger as I do your gold," and he pulled my long yellow curls playfully as he passed on.

The next night we were all assembled on the little pier or jetty which ran out into the sea, with an upright spar fixed at the extreme end. At the beginning was a railed-off space with seats, which he called the family pew. Mr. Dickens was in high spirits, and enjoyed the darkness of the evening, because he escaped the curious eyes of the Broadstairs population. We had a quadrille all to ourselves, the music being Frederick Dickens' whistling, and Mr. Dickens' accompaniment on his pocket-comb. We then strolled farther down to watch by the fading light the tide come rippling in. The night grew darker, starless and moonless; the only light being a lingering lurid gleam, which touched the crests of the waves with a phosphorescent glimmer. Dickens seemed suddenly to be possessed with the demon of mischief; he threw his arm around me and ran me down the inclined plane to the end of the jetty till we reached the tall post. He put his other arm around this, and exclaimed in theatrical tones that he intended to hold me there till " the sad sea-waves " should submerge us.

"Think of the sensation we shall create! Think of the road to celebrity which you are about to tread! No, not exactly to *tread*, but to flounder into!"

Here I implored him to let me go, and struggled hard to release myself.

"Let your mind dwell on the column in the *Times*, wherein will be vividly described the pathetic fate of the lovely E. P., drowned by Dickens in a fit of dementia! Don't struggle, poor little bird; you are powerless in the claws of such a kite as this child!"

By this time the gleam of light had faded out, and the water close to us looked uncomfortably black.

The tide was coming up rapidly and surged over

my feet. I gave a loud shriek, and tried to bring him back to common sense by reminding him that "My dress, my best dress, my *only* silk dress, would be ruined." Even this climax did not soften him; he still went on with his serio-comic nonsense, shaking with laughter all the time, and panting with his struggles to hold me.

"Mrs. Dickens!" a frantic shriek this time, for now the waves rushed up to my knees; "help me! make Mr. Dickens let me go—the waves are up to my knees!"

"Charles!" cried Mrs. Dickens, echoing my wild scream, "how can you be so silly? You will both be carried off by the tide" (tragically, but immediately sinking from pathos to bathos), "and you 'll spoil the poor girl's silk dress!"

"Dress!" cried Dickens, with withering scorn. "Talk not to me of *dress!* When the pall of night is enshrouding us in Cimmerian darkness, when we already stand on the brink of the great mystery, shall our thoughts be of fleshly vanities? Am I not immolating a brand-new pair of patent leathers still unpaid for? Perish such low-born thoughts! In this hour of abandonment to the voice of destiny shall we be held back by the puerilities of silken raiment? Shall leather or prunella (whatever that may be) stop the bolt of Fate?" with a sudden parenthetical sinking from bombast to familiar accents, and back again.

At this point I succeeded in wresting myself free, and scampered to my friends, almost crying with vexation, my *only* silk dress clinging clammily round me, and streaming with salt water. My chaperone, Mrs. S——, received me with unjust severity, evidently thinking I could have got away if I had chosen.

"Run home at once," she said majestically, "and take off your wet things. I am surprised at you!"

During this wrestling match between us, I cannot describe the ridiculous effect produced by his "mouthing" in the Ercles vein, with now and then a quick descent into comicality,—the contrast between the stiltified language and the gasping struggles caused by my efforts to get free, his suppressed chuckles at my dismay, my wild appeals, and the expostulations of his wife and the rest, who stood by, like the chorus in a Greek play, powerless to help.

I went off, escorted by Frederick Dickens, after hearing Mrs. Charles say—

"It was too bad of you, Charles; remember poor E. cannot afford to have her dress destroyed. Of course you'll give her another?"

"Never!" was the reply. "I have sacrificed her finery and my boots to the infernal gods. Kismet! It is finished! Eureka! etc., etc.; and now I go to tug myself black in the face getting off my pedal covers."

Dickens was rather reckless in his fun sometimes, and my wardrobe suffered wofully in consequence. There was a sort of promontory stretching out into the sea, where, in rough weather, the waves used to rush up several feet, and come splashing down like a shower-bath. On two occasions, when I had thoughtlessly ventured near this spot, he seized me and ran me, *nolens volens*, right under the cataract, to the irretrievable ruin of two bonnets of frail fabric, and my slender purse was taxed to the utmost to replace them.

It was arranged that we should make an excursion to Pegwell Bay, and lunch at the small hotel on prawns and bottled porter ; and on a lovely morning two open carriages stood at our door ready to receive us. Mrs. Dickens and two of her lady visitors had walked to our house, and we were only waiting for Mr. Dickens and some gentlemen friends. Presently he came in in high glee, flourishing a yard of ballads, which he had just bought from a beggar in the street.

" Look here ! fair dames and damosels," he cried exultingly. " All for one penny ! invested by yours truly for the delectation of the company. One song alone is worth a Jew's eye,—quite new and original,—the subject being the interesting announcement about our Gracious Queen. It is in the vulgar tongue, but you are all so familiar with ' Nix my Dolly,' and other songs of that kind, that I dare say you will not be shocked."

He commenced to give us a specimen, but after hearing one verse there arose a cry of universal execration. The song was founded on the official notice that a prince or princess might shortly be expected, and was sung to the tune of "The King of the Cannibal Islands." He pretended to be vexed at us "shutting him up," said there "was nothing wrong in it; he had written a great deal worse himself"; and when we were going to enter the carriage he said:

"Now, look here, I give due notice to all and sundry, that I mean to sing that song and a good many of the others during the ride, so those ladies who think them vulgar can go in the other carriage. I am not going to invest my hard-earned penny for nothing."

I was quite certain that Charles Dickens was the last man in the world to shock the modesty of any female, and too much of a gentleman to do anything that was annoying to us, but I thought it was as well to go in the other carriage, and so he had no ladies with him but his wife and Mrs. S———. I was not sorry on the whole to be where I was, as I heard for the next half-hour small portions of those songs wafted on the breeze to us whenever our vehicle approached near them, and the bursts of laughter from ladies and gentlemen, and the mischievous twinkle in Dickens' eye, proved that he was in such a madcap mood that it was as well there were none but married people with him, the subject being what it was, of a "Gampish" nature.

He was not always full of spirits or even-tempered; indeed, I was somewhat puzzled by the variability of his moods. After indulging in the greatest fun and familiarity over-night, we would sometimes meet him walking alone, when he would look at us with lack-lustre eye, and pass on with a hurried "How d' ye do?"

One day he strolled by our window where Milly and I were standing on the balcony. He turned back, "struck" an attitude (in actors' phrase); with one hand on his heart, and the other upraised, he began mouthing:

" ' 'T is my lady, 't is my love. Oh, would I were a glove upon that hand, that I might kiss that cheek.' "

"Which of us do you intend to be the Juliet to your Romeo?" asked Milly.

"Whichever you choose, my little dears," he said nonchalantly, and, touching his hat, sauntered on.

The next morning he came by again, and found us as before, but he only returned a sulky "How do?" and walked by. Of course we knew that he was in the midst of some brain-spinning, and wanted to be alone. I got to understand his face so well that when I saw the preoccupied look I used to pretend not to see him at all, so as to spare him even the trouble of recognizing me, and I found he was all the better pleased.

One night we all went to the Tivoli Gardens, a place in the style of Vauxhall on a small scale. There was a covered portion set apart for dancing, and we saw some very respectable people footing it with great enjoyment. We had a consultation whether it would be very *infra dig.* if the young ones of our party had a private quadrille among themselves, and, as no one knew us, we decided to enjoy ourselves too. Mr. Dickens, meanwhile, walked about, not venturing into the glare of the lights, as his face was too well known for him to preserve his incognito. There was a girl dancing near us, who had long plaited tails of hair down her back, sandaled shoes, and frilled drawers, to whom, by universal acclamation, we affixed the name of Morleena Kenwigs. Dickens was amused at the resemblance, and was making a laughing remark on her, when a man came close to him and stared knowingly and rather offensively in his face. Dickens moved away, but this bore followed him, glowering with all his eyes, and with ears on full cock to catch every stray word. At last Dickens lost patience, and turning suddenly, confronted him, with :

"Pray, sir, are you a native of this place?"

"N—no, sir," stammered the individual.

"Oh, I beg your pardon!" returned Dickens with elaborate politeness. "I fancied I could detect *broad-stares* on your very face."

I need not say that the unhappy wight vanished into the shades of evening.

One morning at his own house Dickens was talking on art to a gentleman present, and they discussed the statue of Venus, which Byron raves about in his "Pilgrimage." Dickens objected to the expressions used by Byron, " Dazzled and drunk with beauty," "The heart *reels* with its fulness," etc., as being an unpoetical metaphor, and said it must have been written tipsily, under the influence of that beverage (gin-and-water) which sometimes inspired this great poet. I defended the verse, and Dickens rose up, pushed his hands through his flowing locks so as to give them their most weird look, turned down his shirt-collar, slapped his brow, and exclaimed, in the Bombastes Furioso style—

"Stand back! I am suddenly seized with the divine afflatus. Don't disturb me till I have given birth to my grand conceptions."

He took out his pencil, and, finding there was no paper in the room, he stalked with grotesquely melodramatic air to the window, and wrote on the white shutter. Frederick Dickens copied the writing afterward for me, and it was as follows :—

LINES, AFTER BYRON, TO E. P——.

" O maiden of the amber-dropping hair,
 May I, Byronically, thy praises utter?
Drunk with *thy* beauty, tell me, may I dare
 To sing thy pæans *borne upon a shutter?*"

My father was a Scottish author of considerable reputation, and had died suddenly at the age of forty-two, of apoplexy, when I was only twelve years old. I lent Mrs. Dickens some volumes of his writings about this time, and she expressed to me how delighted she was in their perusal. In my presence she asked Mr. Dickens to read them. He looked his distaste at the idea, and when she pressed him " just to read one tale, such a beautifully written one, and very short," he turned and walked off abruptly, muttering—"I hate Scotch stories, and every thing else Scotch." I thought this was very unkind to his wife as well as to me, as she was Scotch too. She colored up, but laughed it off.

There were times when we gave Mr. Dickens "a wide berth," and Milly and I have often run round corners to get out of his way, when we thought he was in one of these moods, which we could tell by one glance at his face. His eyes were always like "danger lamps," and warned people to clear the line for fear of collision. We felt we had to do with a genius, and in the throes and agonies of bringing forth his conceptions, we did not expect him to submit to be interrupted by triflers like ourselves: at these times I confess I was horribly afraid of him. I told him so, to his great amusement.

"Why, there's nothing formidable about *me!*"

"Is n't there?" I answered. "You look like a

forest lion with a shaggy mane at these seasons; and I always think of the words—

> ' He roared so loud, and looked so wondrous grim,
> His very shadow dared not follow him.' "

He laughed aloud, and said, "What! do you play shadow to my lion? Nay, then, as Bottom the weaver says, 'I must aggravate my voice, I will roar you as gently as any sucking dove.'" After this I did not feel quite so frightened of him, though I got out of his way all the same.

On another day Milly and I were on the shore in time to see him clambering down some rocks with his brother Fred. They came toward us laughing, and Dickens, pointing to the knees of his trousers, said, " Look at this fresh sacrifice I have laid on your altar! These good pants nearly destroyed by climbing up that precipitous cliff to carve your name in gigantic letters upon a spot where the tide never reaches, so that you may go down to posterity with your name built upon a rock !"

"Did you likewise carve 'Charles Dickens *fecit*'?" asked I.

"No, I did not."

"Then you might as well have scratched my name on the shifting sands, for all the fame I shall ever attain."

They both walked on laughingly, but I never arrived at the truth whether it was Mr. Dickens, or his brother Fred who did the carving. Certainly, there was my name in letters a foot long on the very face of the rock. Fred and I went to look at it a year afterward, and found it still existing.

At last came the sad day when we must leave them, to return to our " local habitations " in smoky London, and I parted with Mr. and Mrs. Dickens with tears of regret. "Never mind, dear," she said in her sweet, caressing way, " we shall all meet again in London."

Alas! we never met again in the same kindly way. Every thing was changed.

When the Dickenses came home we went to luncheon there, and I remarked how preoccupied he looked, how changed in manner. Mrs. S——, who knew him better than I did, was quite prepared to find him different in London from what he was in Broadstairs, but I was very disappointed. I seldom saw him after this, as he was always full of engagements, but Mrs. Dickens I often met at my friend's house. I went one evening intending to spend it with them, and found Mrs. S—— and Milly dressing to go to a small charade party at the Dickens'. Milly immediately proposed to take me with them, but Mrs. S—— said, looking puzzled and uncertain, that she feared Mr. Dickens might think it a liberty! "If it was anybody else but Charles Dickens I should not hesitate an instant, but he is so odd! One never knows how he might take such a thing. Although I am his daughter's godmother, and we are such friends, I cannot do it."

Mrs. S—— mentioned to Mrs. Dickens how greatly it would be to my advantage (being a young artist struggling into notice, and helping to support my mother and sister) if Mr. Dickens would sit to me for his likeness. With that ready good-heartedness which I always found in her, she immediately offered to sit first herself as an inducement to him, which she kindly did. She wished it kept secret from Mr. Dickens, as she proposed to give it to him as a birthday gift, I believe. The portrait was nearly completed, and all who saw it thought it an excellent likeness; it was arranged that I should bring it myself, in case he might suggest any alteration. Accordingly I went to Devonshire Terrace in a cab with my picture, but found Mr. and Mrs. Dickens were out, but were momentarily expected. I was shown into the dining-room, and requested by the domestic to wait, as Mrs. Dickens expected me. The cloth was laid, either for dinner or luncheon. I waited for an hour, and at last I heard the carriage draw up to the door. Mrs. Dickens came to me with her usual kiss, and "so sorry for keeping you waiting." It was raining fast, and her thin boots were wet with only walking from the carriage, so she took them off there and then, and, fancying I was in a state of suspense, she would not wait for her slippers, but went straight into the library to Mr. Dickens with the portrait in her hand. Notwithstanding the closed door, and that I sat far from it at the fire, I could hear the tones of their voices, Mrs. Dickens' expostulatory, Mr. Dickens' imperative. At last she returned, looking flurried, but trying to put the best face on the matter. She made apologies for him, " That he was not very well, and tired. She hoped I would excuse him not being able to see me."

I faltered out, " Does he not like the portrait?"

" He has not had time to look at it properly. Of course he will think it like. You must n't mind, dear, but to tell the truth he is a little grumpy just now; but it will be all right presently. You know a man is always cross when he has been kept without his dinner. Won't you stay?" she added, hesitatingly, and in such a tone that I knew she was *afraid* I might.

I don't know what I answered. I was thoroughly cut up, and wanted to have a " good cry." I broke from her even while she was kissing me and telling me she would write and let me know how he liked it; she slid into my hand a folded piece of green paper, which I knew was a check, and which I purposely dropped as I passed into the hall. She came after me looking very vexed, and put it in my reticule, saying, " For my sake!" Glad to get out of the house, I did not stay to discuss the point, but almost ran into the rain. Round the corner I found an empty cab, and in it I cried to my heart's content all the way home. I never crossed his threshold again.

Whether it was really that Mr. Dickens was hungry and cross; or whether he was annoyed with Mrs. Dickens for having her portrait done without his knowledge; or whether it was because he did not like the picture, I never could discover. "He was so odd," was the only explanation I ever received from the several "mutual" friends to whom I mentioned the affair. Old Mrs. Dickens liked the picture so much that she begged to have it (I was told), and so it ended. It was some salve to my *amour-propre* that I had, in the same spring, a portrait of the Speaker Shaw Lefevre's daughter in the Academy, hung "on the line," and favorably noticed by several of the papers, and that it was considered a "speaking" likeness.

It is not just or satisfactory to depict only one side of any man's character, and Dickens was no faultless monster. A portrait is incomplete if painted (as Queen Elizabeth, of glorious and despotic memory, insisted on being done) without its proper proportion of shadows. To describe Dickens as always amiable, always just, and always in the right, would be simply false and untrue to nature. It is right to soften as much as possible all the hard edges (as artists do their work with a brush called a " sweetener "), and to throw a shade over the shortcomings of a *truly great man*, touching his weakness with a tender and delicate hand, but speaking of his acts as impartially as possible; more especially when he is gone from us into that unknown region where we may be sure all is truth or nothing. After great inward discussion, I feel that I ought to shake off all moral cowardice, and speak of Mr. Dickens as he was to *me*, "nothing extenuate, nor aught set down in malice"; it is only justice to the living to be truthful to the dead. I must entreat my readers to absolve me of any wish to obtrude my small identity in the slightest degree. It is no egotism which makes the pronoun " I " so often repeated in these pages, but the impossibility to detail Dickens' words or acts without also telling what led to them.

The next occasion on which I met Mr. Dickens was at a large ball of nearly two hundred persons, given by a gentleman connected with me by marriage. He came accompanied by Mrs. Dickens, his two brothers, Frederick and Alfred, and Mr. Maclise, the great painter, since dead. Mr. Dickens looked very handsome, and seemed to enjoy himself immensely; but he never danced once with me, and was only coldly polite, which did not increase my enjoyment. He proposed the health of our host at supper, in a short speech, but with such rapid utterance and in so low a tone that I scarcely caught the whole sense of his words.

The only time I ever felt cross with Mrs. Dickens was on this evening. I was engaged to dance with Mr. Maclise, and he was coming forward to claim me, when she interposed and asked him to dance with her. He told her he was engaged to me, but she would take no refusal, and they whirled off together. Frederick said, "What a shame!" and asked me to try and put up with him instead. Both he and his brother Alfred were very attentive to me, and I danced with each repeatedly. Fred told me he thought Charles was acting "very capriciously," and seemed sorry for me, as I took it to heart; but he was "*odd sometimes.*" The evening concluded with "Sir Roger de Coverley," danced in two long *double* rows. It was a sight to see Maclise at one end and Dickens at the other rushing forward alternately, both with long locks flying free. At one part I had to meet and perform the figure with Mr. Dickens, and he unbent a little, giving me something of the old smile, and whirling me round with something of the old familiar style; but, alas! it was only like a ghost of the happy past, and I could have burst out crying. I had been so proud of the notice of so great a man, I had so sunned myself in his smiles, that it was like an untimely frost, come to "nip my buds from blowing."

Next year I was married, after a long engagement, and shortly afterward went to Broadstairs with my husband. I had not expected to see the Dickenses there, as it was late in the season, and I was sure they would have returned. Fred, who was a great friend of my husband, soon found us out, and we were constantly together; but I kept aloof from his brother, and only spoke to him on one occasion during our stay, which was when we went, accompanied by Fred, to the Tivoli Gardens, and Mr. Dickens and his party were there. If I remember rightly, Miss Hogarth danced with my husband and I with Fred, in a few quadrilles made up with their set. Mrs. Dickens was as kind as ever, and "Boz" danced with her and her sister alternately, with as much enjoyment of the fun as any of us.

After this I never saw him but twice again; once at a concert where the lady who afterward became Fred's wife performed on the piano. He was with his wife and Maclise, and favored me with his usual "How d' ye do?" *en passant*. The last time I ever saw him was a few years ago, when he gave a reading of the "Christmas Carol," and he was indeed marvelously changed. Lined in face, and with grizzled beard, but with even more power than ever in expression, the nostril still, like that of the war-horse, dilated and sensitive. I was astonished at the wonderful difference in his voice and utterance, which was now sonorous and emphatic. His long career of reading and acting had completely cured the thickness which I before remarked, and his declamation was no longer hurried.

A great deal has been said about his hearty willingness to help young struggling people, and his kindly feeling for governesses. All I can say is he never helped me, though he had it in his power to do so to a great extent. There was an excellent lady, a friend of Mrs. S——, whom he often met at her house, who supported her step-mother by her salary as a governess, and whom he knew to be a marvel of self-denial, but he never took any notice of her more than politeness required, though she was enthusiastically enraptured with him, and a little extra kindness would have been the sweetest drop in the tasteless cup of her daily avocations. In 1846, when I had been married about four years, a young lady, only seventeen years of age, of very uncommon ability as an artist, implored me to get Mr. Dickens to look at some very clever outline illustrations she had made of his "Chimes" and the "Cricket on the Hearth," hoping to excite his interest in her. I yielded to her solicitations, but, knowing how "odd" Mr. Dickens was, I wrote a letter to Mrs. Dickens requesting her to use her influence with him, and I gave such an account of this young lady's praiseworthy endeavors to earn a livelihood as would, I think, have interested most people. I received this reply from Mrs. Dickens :—

MY DEAR MRS. C. :—Many thanks for your obliging note, and interesting account of your young friend.

Mr. Dickens is so very much occupied just now that he has not as yet been able to look over the drawings, but I have no doubt he will do so very shortly. I trust that yourself and baby are quite well, and that you have good accounts from your husband.

I saw our mutual friends, Mrs. S—— and Miss J——, yesterday.

Excuse this hasty scrawl, and believe me,
My dear Mrs. C——
Very sincerely yours,
CATHERINE DICKENS.

1, DEVONSHIRE TERRACE, 30*th April*, 1846.

My poor little artist was dreadfully disappointed by merely receiving a polite note, thanking her for the sight of her very talented outlines, and that was all. I introduced her shortly after this to my good friend, J. Sidney Cooper, R.A., the eminent cattle-painter, and he invited her to his house to meet people of note and influence, and treated her with such true kindness that she never ceased to thank me. To prove that he must have infinitely benefited her, I have a letter from her sister, written long after, in which she says they had had no chance of getting on till I "used my fairy wand and conjured up that bright circle at Mr. Cooper's for her;

so that, you see, treat the matter as you will, it comes back to *you* at last; Minnie owes her highest encouragement, and both of us some of our best friends, to your active kindness."

The other members of Mr. Dickens' family whom I knew continued always on the same terms, and a few years ago Fred came, accompanied by his father-in-law, and stayed some days with us. After that he came with Mrs. S——, and remained with us a week, and he would never admit that his brother felt unkindly toward me, though he could not explain his strange conduct.

The last I ever had to do with Mr. Dickens was when I wrote to ask the favor of a few lines from him in support of an appeal I was about to make to a statesman high in office on behalf of the aged and necessitous widow of an author of repute formerly; but he declined in a few curt sentences, on the grounds that I had been "absurdly misinformed" as to his having any influence in such quarter.

The following article is extracted from *Lippincott's Magazine:*

### WITH DICKENS—AT THE BANQUET-BOARD AND ON SHIPBOARD.

I had secured my passage in the *Scotia*, which was to leave Liverpool on November 2d, and was spending a week in London prior to the day of sailing. In my quiet lodgings in Sackville Street I had heard no news; so it was with interest, and some vexation, that I saw one morning in the *Times* the announcement that a farewell banquet, to be given to Charles Dickens previous to his departure for America, was to come off on the evening of November 2d.

For a moment I was completely dispirited at remembering I should be leaving the British Channel at that very hour. There were only three days to elapse, and I could not reasonably expect the steamship company to transfer my state-room on so short a notice; and, besides, there was no assurance of a ticket to the dinner at this late hour. Yet to miss such an occasion without an effort was not to be thought of. I hastened into Piccadilly, to the nearest cab-stand, and on lifting my finger a hansom wheeled from the line and brought up at the curb in a twinkling.

I drove straight to the publishers' who held the tickets. In answer to my application a clerk said the number had to be limited to five hundred, and they had all been taken on the first announcement.

"I am very desirous of going; is there no chance for me between now and then?"

The only encouragement he gave me was to add fuel to the flame of my desire by saying, with considerable fervor: "This is a very remarkable occasion; there will probably be assembled at Freemasons' Tavern a greater number of distinguished people than were ever under one roof before."

"Yes, I know," I interrupted, "and possibly out of that great number there will be some one who can't go; in which case I beg you to secure the place for me."

And then I pleaded my nationality in a faint-hearted way, with the feeble hope that it might beguile him into making an effort for me. He opened a blank-book at this, and showed me that nineteen applicants for such chances had been ahead of me. "But I'll put you down for the twentieth, if you wish," he said, in a tone that left no room for hope.

I left the shop, determined to remain in London and trust to luck, if I could do so without sacrificing my passage. A telegram was at once sent to Liverpool, asking the favor of a transfer to the *Cuba*, which was to sail a week later. Then, having dismissed the cab, I strolled along the Strand as far as Wellington Street, when it occurred to me that possibly some clerk in the office of *All the Year Round* might be in possession of a ticket and be indifferent about using it; but I was told there was no chance outside the publishing house. Into the Strand again I pushed along, not yet quite disheartened. There must be some way open for one so bent on admission, I thought—some magic words to open the door of this Freemasons' cave. "Let me see—'Open wheat,' 'Open rye!' Open—open *guineas!*"

In two minutes more I was again in a hansom, driving smartly for the publishers'.

"Open wheat, open rye," I murmured to the clerk.

"No one has yet returned a ticket," he responded.

"Open guineas!" I exclaimed. Whereupon, after consultation with a brother clerk, he said to me: "It's possible one may turn up by evening; and if it should, I'll send a note to your lodgings."

I thanked him, drove away, and—well, I got the ticket! Somebody from the country, I think, who could n't come to town on that evening. The following telegram soon justified my venture, and put me in everlasting good-humor with the steamship company: "Berth cancelled, and transferred to *Cuba.*"

Out of the fog and into the crowded cloak-room of Freemasons' Hall I stepped before the clock struck seven. A letter *B* on my dinner-card denoted the section to which the holder was assigned; so, when the ushers invited section *B*, I followed a number up to the banquet-hall, where five hundred Britons, in dress-coats and white cravats, were taking their seats at the long tables. The dinner committee, composed of Wilkie Collins, Fechter, and other personal friends of Dickens, were so business-like in their arrangements that the throng fell into their places with the greatest ease and order. While awaiting the arrival of the guest, I had leisure to observe the apartment and the people about me. In each panel on the walls was inscribed in gold letters the title of one of Mr. Dickens' most famous works. It was pleasant to watch the countenances of his countrymen as they read with new ardor these titles—to see them lighten with interest or broaden into smiles as the immortal names of "Nicholas," "The Christmas Carol," "David," and "Pickwick" met their eyes.

It is not hard to detect a stranger; so my table companion, assuring himself of my case, politely offered to point out any lions that might be in sight, either couchant or prowling about. Men were passing quickly from one table to the other, talking in high good-humor. "Do you see that stout man who has just left his seat?" The man described stopped near us, and, leaning over, began to tell something with immense glee to a listening group seated at table—stout of body and big of head, with uncommon spirit and animation. "That's Mark Lemon," my friend said as he turned from them shaking with laughter. How well his name fits his office! I thought, as I saw for the first and last time the editor of *Punch*, in the not inappropriate function of being the spirit of mirth at a banquet.

At this moment something like an announcement was heard at the door; a stir was in the room, and the whole assemblage rose and broke into applause.

Mr. Dickens entered, accompanied by Lord Lytton, and followed by a score of gentlemen. Very serious was his expression as he walked by the ranks of men clapping their hands vehemently. He seemed to be striving to keep down the emotion caused by this warm reception, and looked neither to right nor left as he traversed the long room. Bulwer walked close at his elbow, and while the applause deepened looked about him as if in a picture-gallery, stroked his beard, and threw his glances indifferently around, now on the people, now up at the inscriptions, as though he would say, " I am determined not to appear to accept one grain of this applause for myself."

A minute, and they had passed, the group of eminent men crowding after so quickly that only a few could be named for me : " The lord chief-justice, who is sure to speak. The somewhat spare man, carrying his head bent, is Sir Charles Lyell, the geologist. That large man, nearly seven feet high, is 'Jacob Omnium' of the *Times*, one of Thackeray's friends. And there is Sir Edwin Landseer." Amazing ! I thought, as I looked upon the old man who half a century ago painted Dandie Dinmont's terriers, Pepper and Mustard. My companion brought me abruptly out of the past by exclaiming : " Look quickly if you would see the handsomest man in England—the man with no beard, just passing ! That 's Millais, the artist."

I looked, and saw one of the noted trio of Pre-Raphaelites. His face is indeed uncommonly handsome, and not of the florid English type. But I thought, as they hurried by, that they all looked somewhat low-spirited—like men who had been waiting longer than usual for dinner.

Lord Lytton occupied the chair, with Mr. Dickens on his right and the lord chief-justice on his left. Behind the chair was the royal standard crossed with the stars and stripes, above which was a wreath encircling the monogram of the guest; while surmounting these, and almost directly over the head of the author, were the glittering letters that form the magic name of "Pickwick."

And now the clink of soup-plates peals a welcome alarum, and the Army, the Navy, the Bench, and the Bar, princes, potentates, and warriors, fall to with great alacrity. Oh, the clatter, the murmur, the hum of a great dinner! What a sight is that of five hundred men feeding at table! How pleasant to observe the measureless content that rests upon each countenance!

"Stick to the claret, for the sherry at these public dinners is always risky," said my neighbor. I obeyed him, and with the aid of certain glees and madrigals that were sung at intervals, made the time pass till the main business was reached. This was entered on by ceremoniously getting through the usual loyal toasts and offering congratulations to the royal family.

There is one wholesome practice which prevails in England that must always startle an American when he witnesses it for the first time. It is that of coughing down a speaker who is becoming prosy. Accustomed to our own social timidity, that compels us patiently to endure the droning of some diffusive bore through a long hour, one is astounded when a whole audience is taken with a violent catarrhal trouble, that makes such a clamor as to drown the speaker and force him to capitulate. On this occasion, after the British flag had been waved long enough, and over barbarous Abyssinia in particular, a certain Captain Somebody of the Navy kept on carrying it round the world, with a running talk on ships and naval reforms generally. A shot or two having no effect, he received a broadside which sunk him at once, and silence for a moment settled over him. The same fate awaited Mr. Tom Taylor, the dramatic writer. Having been for some years actively interested in the organization and drill of volunteer rifle companies, it fell to his lot to return thanks for the toast to the volunteers. Hearty cheers awarded his earlier remarks, which were pertinent and telling, but instead of wisely stopping, he diffused his critical observations over such a wide surface that he had to be admonished by a scathing fire. Heedless of this, he went on, all reason having apparently fled, and fatuously strove to withstand the tremendous volley which now assailed him. He staggered for an instant, and then dropped into his seat.

Arriving now at the chief toast of the evening, the chairman arose and began to address the eager company. At first we could hear no more than some vocal sounds, but presently could distinguish some inflections of voice. Lord Lytton was manifestly speaking, for he was making gestures and uttering sounds, and everybody was trying to hear his words, but without success. There sat several hundred men with their faces aslant, intently and respectfully listening to an inarticulate gurgle. His voice was not weak, and he used it with some force and deliberation, but he seemed to be engaged in swallowing his words as fast as they were formed. Now and then his arms would move and his slender body swing forward and backward with the energy of his thought. If a word was caught, the meaning of a sentence was conjectured, and applause would follow. Then drawing himself erect, as if he thought all his eloquent remarks were distinctly heard, he would lift high his narrow shoulders, as though gathering for a fresh burst. And when it came, my attentive ear was obliged to turn away baffled. Upon pointedly addressing a gentleman who sat near him at table, it was obvious to some that he was making a direct appeal to Matthew Arnold in support of some proposition that never had an audible existence. But it required the morning journals afterward to tell us that Bulwer addressed him as "one distinguished for the manner in which he has brought together all that is most modern in sentiment with all that is most scholastic in thought and language."

We furthermore had it verified that his oration was a glowing panegyric on Dickens, to whom he turned on closing and looked down upon him. Aided by this action, we could gather that he proposed "a prosperous voyage, health, and long life to our illustrious guest and countryman, Charles Dickens."

Mr. Dickens was on his feet in an instant, and in that voice now so well known, with the least touch of huskiness in it, confessed that the composure which he was used to command before an audience was so completely shaken that he could only hope they might see in him now "some traces of an eloquence more expressive than the richest words." It was not alone owing to the deep stillness and the close attention of the audience that every word he spoke was so readily heard. His voice was not sonorous, nor did he employ what commonly passes for elocution, but by a distinct and forcible enunciation, and putting a slight stress upon a suggestive word, often at the close of a sentence, he would drive it home to the hearer, laden with all the meaning he intended, and sometimes perhaps more than the printed text would suggest.

In a bold figure, while referring to the emotions which his reception by this great assemblage aroused, he said : " The wound in my breast, dealt to me by the hands of my friends, is deeper than the soundless sea and wider than the whole catholic church!" The intense energy and dramatic fervor with which this was uttered sent a thrill through the entire company. Yet considerable laughter immediately followed, showing that the sentiment was extravagant enough to be regarded as a *bon mot.* He told them of "the great pressure of American invitations, and of the hearty and homely expressions of personal affection for him which it would be dull insensibility in him not to prize." Further, he promised to use his best endeavors "to lay down a third cable of intercommunication between the Old World and the New."

As this was a company of Englishmen, it was no doubt in excellent taste for the speaker to say the following words of the nation he was about to visit: "I know full well that whatever little motes my beamy eyes may have descried in theirs, they are a kind, large-hearted, generous, and great people." But somehow I was a little uncomfortable under this, and, though quite unwarrantably, felt as if I were a representative, a sort of accidental ambassador, with imputed national sensibilities. The very folds of our flag that hung there seemed to become sentient, and indeed capable of hearing what was said. But this little conceit speedily gave place to a pang of regret as the address was now about to end. With the quotation from that wise little atomy, Tiny Tim, of "God bless us every one!" Mr. Dickens resumed his seat.

There was a moment of stillness before any applause, and the company maintained their listening attitude, reluctant to part with him. Mr. Trollope, soon following, sensibly limited himself to few words, and those were in denunciation of a certain prophet of our day, whose bitter lamentations were unnecessary and disagreeable. Mr. Trollope was sufficiently lucid for everybody to know that he meant Thomas Carlyle. It was in this eccentric mode he returned thanks for the toast to Literature. The closing address by the lord chief-justice, looked to with interest, was a fulsome panegyric on the chairman. Lord Lytton was lolling his fatigued frame in an arm-chair, with his head on one side as if asleep. The orator talked to him and at him. Standing close at his side, he seemed, even by the gestures of his hands, to be baling out eulogy and deluging Bulwer with it. But the statesman-novelist never once moved his tired head. If, as is said, Bulwer is so deaf that he could not hear a word of it, the situation becomes ludicrous. The banquet was over, and the scene shifted to London streets.

Early on the following Saturday morning I went on board a little ferry-boat at the Liverpool wharf, and deposited my hat-box at the foot of a huge, pyramidal pile of luggage that stood on the centre of the deck. The things had been hastily heaped together, and the pile was crowned by another hat-box, which was rendered unsteady by the motion of the boat. Presently it toppled, and after making one or two ill-considered movements, rolled steadily to the bottom, where it was arrested by my own hat-box, against which it leaned trustingly. On its lid was painted in large black letters the name "Charles Dickens." This little incident informed us of the precious freight the *Cuba* was to carry, and was read as a happy augury of a pleasant ocean voyage.

"That's him now, a-coming down the plank," said a rough-looking man to a knot of others. Approaching the tug at a fast walk was a man of medium height, with weather-beaten, ruddy face and light blue eyes. He was dressed in a heavy, double-breasted pea-jacket, and wore a Derby hat. It is the first mate hastening aboard, I should have said had I not seen him before. This apparently seafaring man was the only passenger to whom anxious farewells were said ; and as a rosy young girl clung tearfully about his neck in daughterly fashion, the rigging became suddenly interesting to me, and my note-book was closed.

When fairly on our way it was apparent that Mr. Dickens' known pedestrian habits were invincible by wind or wave. To and fro, between the wheel-house and the smoke-stack, he paced the deck for hours every day. These walks were mostly alone, for the reserve with which he obviously sheltered himself was respected from beginning to end. It was only in those accidental encounters or inevitable juxtapositions arising on shipboard that he was addressed by his fellow-passengers. But he rarely spoke first, save in the morning salutation on deck. He never once joined the shivering group that clustered about the smoke-stack for warmth, but paced and paced, engaged apparently in serious thought.

"I wish he would begin to lay the cable now," thought I, "according to his promise at the banquet; it would be such an excellent chance while he has us here so handy on shipboard." But night fell and day rose, mists drove and the sun shone, and the steamer went booming along, and the passengers chatted and walked and ate and drank, and still the great envoy made no sign of laying the cable.

It was the most natural thing in the world for everybody aboard to want to say something to him. And what could be more natural than that the restraint, which was self-imposed out of consideration for his comfort, should give way on the least provocation? There, walking back and forth daily among them, went the man who had probably given them more pleasure and delight than any other living, had cheered them in calamity, had heightened their joys, had cleared their vision to see the beauty and goodness that may lie in common surroundings, and created a gratitude in their hearts that cannot be measured. So in the course of three or four days all had a speaking acquaintance with him, and whoever joined him found him easy of approach and not averse to talk.

"I have knocked about the Channel a good deal, and have learned in that way," he explained to one who marvelled at his knowledge of sailor-craft. Whenever the heavy tramp of the gang was heard as the men reeled in the wet log-line, there stood Mr. Dickens watching it as it was pulled tight and dripping along the deck. Among the first to know what run the ship had made, few could ever carry him the news, spite of the uncertain hours at which the log was heaved. How distinctly I recall his figure as he climbed up the ladder to the deck! First his low-crowned, round hat appeared; then his ruddy face lit with his marvellously blue eyes; then his double-breasted seaman's coat. On sunny days he would carry up in his hand a huge book bound in blue. On the cover was stamped a gilt picture of an elephant with uplifted trunk chasing a boy. It was a book on India. He would place this big volume on a bulkhead or bench, and sit down by it as if he contemplated reading. But he never read a page of it while on deck. His quick glance was up at the sails, the mystery of ropes, the clouds, the way of the wind, and everywhere but on the book.

On a day when the ship rolls heavily men's faces are often portentously long at dinner in the saloon. "If I could only keep my feet till the bell rings, I should get safely through," I observed one day.

"Take hot negus for lunch : it will keep you up much better than the ale," Mr. Dickens replied. Then, pursuing the subject, he said : "My worst time is in the morning when I get up : how do you manage then ?"

"Watch the towels, and the moment they stop swinging make a dive for the lounge, seize my flask and take one spoonful of brandy."

"But only one ; for if you take more," he said, curving one eyebrow and smiling, "you are defeated. That's my plan also, and it works very well."

Of course I prized hints from this source, especially as they had a smack of the "Markis o' Granby" and the "Maypole." The chat turned on travel, on winter climates, went back to Europe, trundled down to Italy and his long residence at Genoa, and the beauty of the Riviera. The lovely features of the Cornice were tossed from hand to hand, as though we were capping verses. "How picturesque those villages !" said he. "And what a balmy air !" exclaimed another. "And that blue sea in front!" pursued Dickens. "And the shining orange groves!" "Yes, and backed with those rich hills!" he added with almost lyric fervor. At this moment a new-comer broke in with some odious remark about the number of "knots she's running." He flung his great cobble-stone into the smooth flow of talk, and there was an end of it.

One evening I was sitting alone on deck while teapots and lighted candles were being placed in the saloon below. Some one was climbing up the ladder, and I perceived the outlines of Mr. Dickens' hat and coat. He took a camp-stool and sat near me. After a word or two we travelled ahead of the ship to America.

"How far is it from New York to Philadelphia? or, rather, how long is it? for it's absurd in these days to ask how far." After the comforting assurance that it was only three hours and a half, I asked him whether he remembered a certain venerable lady of Philadelphia whom he had met when here before. He said: "Perfectly well; indeed I never *forget any thing!*" and repeated with some emphasis that he had a great memory.

He knew the capacity of the opera-houses in the Eastern cities, and remarked that he preferred a small or medium-sized hall to read in—"a room in which everybody can see my face," he said, "for so much depends on the face and the lighter shades of voice."

"What do you mean by a *good* audience?" he asked.

"*Good* refers to size rather than quality, and mostly means a full house."

At this moment a lady, wrapped in a water-proof and hood, came up and sat down on the deck by us. And then arose questions about Miss Adelaide Procter and other writers.

"Did you know Mrs. Browning?" asked the lady passenger.

"Oh, yes, indeed!"

"Do tell me something about her!"

"Well, she was one of the smallest women you ever saw, and was ill a good deal. It was very funny to see the way Browning used to carry her about all over Europe." The talk fell on Browning's plays "Colombe's Birthday" and "The Blot in the 'Scutcheon "—" that remarkable thing in literature, a tragedy without a crime!" somebody said. Mr. Dickens warmly assented to the praise given to the dramatic fragment.

"Notwithstanding its beauty, I suppose Browning never intended it to be acted?" asked one.

"Oh, yes," he replied; "Browning requested me once to fit it for the stage, and I did so. It was not the fault of the play that it was not successful; it was because the audiences were not up to it."

However skeptical I may have felt about this criticism, I said nothing, and Mr. Dickens expressed still further his admiration of Browning. He asked me if I had read the poem "Rabbi Ben Ezra." I had not, whereupon he commended it warmly, and advised me to read it.

I had but one more talk with him, and that a brief one. One afternoon, during a walk together on deck, I said: "Mr. Dickens, if you don't object to my asking you something about your books—"

"Not at all," he said, cordially.

"I would ask you to give me a word to characterize certain qualities which the style assumes occasionally." I hated, I said, to employ the word melodramatic, feeling it to be inappropriate, but could find no other, and asked if he objected to it in any case.

"What do you mean when you say melodramatic?" he inquired.

"When the style rises above the level of common prose, and the sentiment lifts itself out of the region of common things, and the sentences actually become rhythmical. There is something of it in 'the storm' in 'David'"—he nodded affirmatively,—"in 'An Italian Dream' in the 'Pictures from Italy,' the chapters on 'Monseigneur' in the 'Tale of Two Cities' possess it; and the passages wherein Lucie Manette hears the echoes of hurrying footsteps where no footsteps are, are all musical and suggestive of more than they say."

"Yes, I recognize—I understand you perfectly;

but that which you mean I should not call melodramatic : I call it *picturesque.*"

Then dwelling on this for a moment, " Let me tell you," he said, " the definition I gave to an English artist the other day, who asked me to explain the difference between the theatrical and the dramatic in a picture. I said, 'If any of the figures in the scene look as if they thought they were being looked at, if their expression in the least shows them to be aware of spectators, I should call it theatrical. But when they do their part with unconscious energy, and are wholly subject to the governing emotions of the scene, it is dramatic.' "

He was elaborating this definition, when a large man joined us and put his clumsy foot into the talk and trampled it shapeless.

When within sixty miles of Boston a pilot-boat came tossing around, with a pilot in her dressed in black cassimere trousers, a neat overcoat, and heavy kid gloves. The first question he asked as he reached the deck was whether Mr. Dickens was on board.

And now we took our last dinner, the captain's dinner ; at the close of which Mr. Dickens agreeably surprised the company by making a spirited little speech, and proposing the health of the captain in such genial words as to overcome that officer's wonted taciturnity. A few hours after this we were in Boston Harbor, where a band of gentlemanly marauders boarded the steamer, seized their prize, and bore him away.

## CHAPTER XVI.

### WILLIAM MAKEPEACE THACKERAY.

*Was he a cynic?—Anecdotes of his benevolence and kindness—His appearance in society—John Esten Cooke's memoranda of an hour's conversation—Charlotte Brontë's impressions of Thackeray.*

IN a pleasant paper in *Appletons' Monthly*, called "An Hour with Thackeray," Mr. John Esten Cooke tells us that, having been invited to pay a call upon the great English novelist while he was stopping in Richmond, his first impression was one of surprise at the remarkable difference between the real man and the malicious cartoons of him drawn by his English critics. These gentlemen seemed to have dipped their pens in gall before drawing his likeness. Their outlines were bit in with acid. There had never lived, according to them, a more unamiable human being than the author of "Vanity Fair." Persons with any respect for themselves could not endure him. His heart was cold, his disposition cyni-

cal, and his manners so haughty and repelling that everybody thrown in contact with him became his enemy. As he strode by, he scarcely deigned to return the salutes of his friends, if he had any. He would stare, or respond with a curt nod. He would sit up hobnobbing with intimates until four in the morning, and then pass the same persons in the afternoon, as he rode toward the Park, with a movement of the head so cold and indifferent that it quite froze them. He rarely smiled; had nothing about him either natural or inviting; to quote the words of one of his critics: "His bearing is cold and uninviting, his style of conversation either openly cynical or affectedly good-natured and benevolent; his *bonhomie* is forced, his wit biting, his pride easily touched." As to his character, that was said to be as disagreeable as his manners. "He was one mass of gloom and misanthropy. Cynicism was his philosophy and contempt his religion. A mixture of Timon and Diogenes, he went about with a scowl on his brow and a sneer on his lips, refusing to see good anywhere, and spitting out his hate and venom on the whole human species." This was the sort of man he had expected to see, and he was surprised, therefore, to find in his place "a tall, ruddy, simple-looking Englishman, who cordially held out his hand, and met me with a friendly smile. There was nothing like a scowl on the face, and it was neither thin, bilious, nor ill-natured, but plump, rubicund, and indicative of an excellent digestion. His voice was neither curt nor ungracious, but courteous and cordial—the voice of a gentleman receiving a friend under his own roof. In person he was a 'large man'—his height I think was above six feet. His eyes were mild in expression, his hair nearly gray, his dress plain and unpretending. Every thing about the individual produced the impression that pretence was hateful to him. He was quiet in his manner, and spoke slowly and deliberately in a low tone—apparently uttering his thought as it rose to his lips without selecting his words. After spending ten minutes with him, it was easy to see that he was a man of the world in the best sense of the phrase, and neither a bitter Juvenal nor a shy 'literary man,' living only in books. There was, indeed, almost nothing of the typical *littérateur* about him. His face and figure indicated a decided fondness for roast beef, canvas-back ducks—of which he spoke in terms of enthusiasm,—plum-pudding, 'Bordeaux,'—of which he told me he drank a bottle daily at his dinner,—and all the material good things of life. The idea of a disordered liver seems absurd in connection with him. The fact is, Mr. Thackeray was a *bon vivant*—not given to wearing his heart upon his sleeve, but prone to goodfellowship, fond of his ease, and liked nothing better than to loll in his arm-chair, tell or listen to a good story, sing a good song, smoke a good cigar, and 'have his talk out' with his chosen friends.

As to the general tone of his conversation, what impressed me most forcibly was his entire unreserve, and the genuine *bonhomie* of his air—a *bonhomie* which struck me as being any thing but what his critic, Mr. Yates, called it—'forced.' The man seemed wholly simple and natural, and I could fancy him saying: 'I have nothing to conceal from you, friend; you see me just as I am, and you are welcome to use your strongest magnifying-glasses to discover any hidden humbug about me, and to drag it forth and denounce it publicly. I say what I think, and am not trying to make any impression upon you, good or bad. My desire is to be friendly and natural, avoiding what is hateful to me—sham and deceit.' He smiled easily, and evidently enjoyed the humorous side of things, but in private, as in delivering his lectures on Swift and some others, there was an undertone of sadness in his voice."

Thackeray was a man of the world, to be sure, and one whom experience of the world had thoroughly disillusioned, but the well of natural tenderness was never dried in his heart. "He rejoiced," says Bayard Taylor, "with a fresh boyish delight, in every evidence of an unspoiled nature in others, in every utterance which may have seemed to him overfaith in the good. The more he was saddened by his knowledge of human weakness and folly, the more gratefully he welcomed strength, virtue, sincerity. His eyes never unlearned the habit of that quick moisture which honors the true word and noble deed."

All who were ever admitted to the confidence of this great and tender-hearted genius have their own stories to tell of his noble generosities and kindnesses and acts of quiet benevolence.

To give some immediate pleasure, Mr. Trollope says, was the great delight of his life—a sovereign to a school-boy, gloves to a girl, a dinner to a man, a compliment to a woman. His charity was overflowing, his generosity excessive. "I heard once a story of woe from a man who was the dear friend of both of us. The gentleman wanted a large sum of money instantly—something under two thousand pounds,—had not natural friends who could provide it, but must go utterly to the wall without it. Pondering over this sad condition of things, I met Thackeray, and told him the story. 'Do you mean to say I am to find two thousand pounds?' he said, angrily, with some expletives. I explained that I had not even suggested the doing of any thing—only that we might discuss the matter. Then there came over his face a peculiar smile and a wink in his eye, and he whispered his suggestion, as though half ashamed of his meanness: 'I'll go half,' he said, 'if anybody will go the rest.' And he did go half, at a day or two's notice, though the gentleman was no more than simply a friend. I am glad to be able to add that the money was quickly repaid." There are current many other anecdotes of the same kind. A friend entering Thackeray's bedroom in Paris found him placing some napoleons in a pill-box, on the lid of which was written, "One to be taken occasionally." When questioned as to what he was doing, "Well," he replied, "there is an old person here who says she is very ill, and I strongly suspect that this is the sort of medicine she wants. Dr. Thackeray intends to leave it with her himself. Let us walk out together."

Blanchard Jerrold was one morning at Horace Mayhew's chambers in Regent Street, when a knock was heard at the door, and a voice cried from without: "It's no use, Porry Mayhew; open the door."

"It's dear old Thackeray," said Mayhew, instinctively putting chairs and table in order to do honor to the friend of whom he never spoke without pride.

Thackeray came in, saying cheerily: "Well, young gentlemen, you'll admit an old fogy."

He always spoke of himself as an old man, says Jerrold. Between him and Mayhew there were not many years. He took up the papers lying about, talked the gossip of the day, and then suddenly said—with his hat in his hand—"I was going away without doing part of the business of my visit. You spoke the other day at the dinner [the *Punch* weekly meeting] of poor George. Somebody—most unaccountably—has returned me a five-pound note I lent him a long time ago. I did n't expect it: so just hand it to George; and tell him, when his pocket will bear it, to pass it on to some poor fellow of his acquaintance. By-bye." A nod and he was gone.

The reason that Thackeray's real nature was so generally misunderstood by his cotemporaries is not far to seek. He was a reaction against the spirit of his age. He came upon the world at the time when the grotesque sham into which Byronism had degenerated at the hands of Byron's admirers was emasculating literature; when the Great Soul was the popular ideal,—the gifted, gloomy, mysterious being who did not love the world nor the world him, but who usually had an amiable weakness for the world's wife. He was a protest against all this. He was a protest, too, against the rampant egotism that found its fullest expression in the fiction of that period, in the earlier novels, for instance, of Bulwer and Disraeli, mere clever *poseurs* without any earnestness or sincerity, who were continually proclaiming their own merits from the house-tops, and inviting public attention to the beauty of their own emotions. In the vigor of his protest against all this brag and bluster, Thackeray may have gone to the opposite extreme. A man who is anxious to keep straight is liable to bend over on the opposite side. So, in the reaction against unreal enthusiasms Thackeray habitually talked under what he felt. He veiled his deeper feelings beneath a self-respecting reticence; he would have shrunk from making public exhibition of the pulsations of a troubled heart. A friend who knew him and valued him, and who tells us that in the discussion of serious subjects he was apt, when pressed, to have recourse to banter, acknowledges that much of his light talk was intended not so much to conceal as to keep down a sensibility amounting almost to womanliness which belonged to his nature, and which contrasted, one might almost say struggled, with the manliness which was equally its characteristic. "He could not read any thing pathetic without actual discomfort, and was unable, for example, to go through with the 'Bride of Lammermoor.' I have heard him allude to some early sorrows, especially the loss of a child, in a way which showed how sharp and painful was the recollection after the lapse of many years. That he could sympathize warmly with others I infer from much that I have heard. His well-known sensitiveness sprung perhaps from the same root as his sensibility. 'I like Thackeray,' an English critic once said in my hearing, 'but I cannot respect him—he is so sensitive.' But his sensitiveness made harsh things distasteful to him even when he was not himself the object of them. 'You fiend!' he said to a friend who was laughing over a sharp attack on an acquaintance of both, and refused to hear or read a word of it."

A story told by Mr. Hodder, who was for some years Thackeray's private secretary, seems to me to shed a great deal of light upon the real tenderness of heart that lay beneath that cynic exterior.

" On the morning of his departure for America," says Hodder, "he was to start by an early train, and when I arrived (for it had been previously arranged that I should see him before he left) I found him in his study, and his two daughters in the dining-room—all in a very tearful condition; and I do not think I am far wrong in saying that if ever man's strength was overpowered by woman's weakness, it was so upon this occasion; for Mr. Thackeray could not look at his daughters without betraying a moisture in his eyes, which he in vain strove to conceal. Nevertheless he was enabled to attend to several money transactions which it was necessary he should arrange before leaving; and to give me certain instructions about the four volumes of his 'Miscellanies' then in course of publication, and which he begged me to watch in their passage through the press, with a view to a few foot-notes that might be thought desirable. Then came the hour for parting! A cab was at the door, the luggage had all been properly disposed of, and the servants stood in the hall, to notify, by their looks, how much they regretted their master's departure. 'This is the moment I have dreaded!' said Thackeray, as he entered the dining-room to embrace his daughters; and when he hastily descended the steps of the door he *knew* that they would be at the window to

'Cast one longing, lingering look behind.'

' Good-by,' he murmured, in a suppressed voice, as I followed him to the cab; 'keep close behind me, and let me try to jump in unseen.'

"The instant the door of the vehicle was closed behind him, he threw himself back into a corner and buried his face in his hands."

"Let me try to jump in unseen"—that is an eminently characteristic expression. Even in that moment of sorrow he was fearful lest some passer-by should observe his weakness. This was not the temper of mind of (for instance) Dickens. There was a theatrical element in *his* nature, which would have been gratified, I fancy, at finding himself the central figure in a touching scene. The famous "Put that in my biography," in his letter to Forster, recurs to the mind with ugly persistence. And I am quite sure that M. Victor Hugo would have been delighted to bring his whole family before the footlights, and would have solemnly embraced them one by one and accepted the plaudits of the gallery with a pleased sense of deserving them.

And yet Thackeray did not shun the world's eye; on all subjects but that of his own emotions he was perfectly frank and open. He was of much too healthy a mind, we are told, to fear to walk about in his habit as he lived in private, and he never shrouded himself in mysteries, nor broke upon his friends, at stated seasons, in a blaze of glory. He had a delightful habit of taking all he met into his confidence, of telling them his "little miseries"— how discourteous were some of the small enemies who attacked him; how unreasonable were the small friends who besieged him. Of his literary life he spoke with refreshing frankness. "They have only bought so many of my new book." "Have you seen the abuse of my last number?" "What am I to turn my hand to? they are getting tired of my novels." These are given by Trollope as samples of his utterances in open company. And we may be sure that they were not spoken querulously, but with a chuckle of amusement at his own expense. "The gravity of that white head," says James Hannay, "with its noble brow, and thoughtful face full of feeling and meaning, enhanced the piquancy of his playfulness, and of the little personal revelations which came with such a grace from the depths of his kindly nature. When we congratulated him, many years ago, on the touch in 'Vanity Fair' in which Becky *admires* her husband when he is giving Lord Steyne the chastisement which ruins *her* for life, 'Well,' he said, 'when I wrote the sentence, I slapped my fist on the table, and said, *that* is a touch of genius!' The incident is a trifle, but it will reveal, we suspect, an element of fervor, as well as a heartiness of frankness in recording the fervor, both equally at variance with the vulgar conception of him. This frankness and *bonhomie* made him delightful in a *tête-à-tête*, and gave a pleasant human flavor to talk full of sense, and wisdom, and experience, and lighted up by the gaiety of the true London man of the world."

I have already quoted a paragraph from a

paper by Mr. Cooke, and as it affords a good example of the frank and genial manner in which the great writer was wont to speak of himself and his performances, I subjoin the remainder of it here.

### AN HOUR WITH THACKERAY.

Having no business to engage me one morning, I went to call on him at his hotel, and found him in his private parlor, lolling in an easy-chair, and smoking. This good or bad habit, as the reader pleases, was a favorite one with him. He was a dear lover of his cigar, and I had presented him with a bundle of very good small " Plantations," which he afterward spoke highly of, lamenting that his friend G. P. R. James, then consul at Richmond, *would* come and smoke them all. On this morning he had evidently nothing to occupy him, and seemed ready for a friendly talk. Smoking was the first topic, and he said :

" I am fond of my cigar, you see. I always begin writing with one in my mouth."

" After breakfast, I suppose ? I mean that you probably write in the forenoon ? "

" Yes, the morning is my time for composing I can't write at night. I find it excites me so that I cannot sleep."

"May I ask if you ever dictate your books to an amanuensis ? " I said. " I ask this question, Mr.

Thackeray, because our friend Mr. G. P. R. James says that the power to dictate is born with people. If it is not a natural gift, he says it can not be acquired."

"I don't know," Mr. Thackeray replied. "I have dictated a good deal. The whole of 'Esmond' was dictated to an amanuensis."

"I should not have supposed so—the style is so terse that I would have fancied you *wrote* it. 'Esmond' is one of the greatest favorites among your works in this country. I always particularly liked the chapter where Esmond returns to Lady Castlewood, 'bringing his sheaves with him,' as she says."

"I am glad it pleased you. I wish the whole book was as good. But we can't play first fiddle all the time."

"You dictated this chapter?"

"Yes—the whole work. I also dictated all of 'Pendennis.' I can't say I think much of 'Pendennis'—at least of the execution. It certainly drags about the middle, but I had an attack of illness about the time I reached that part of the book, and could not make it any better than it is."

Another allusion to "Esmond," and his portrait of Marlborough, brought from Mr. Thackeray's lips, in a musing tone, the single word "Rascal!" and he then inquired in a very friendly manner what I had written. I informed him, and he said:

"Well, if I were you, I would go on writing—some day you will write a book which will make your fortune. Becky Sharp made mine. I married early, and wrote for bread ; and ' Vanity Fair ' was my first successful work. I like Becky in that book. Sometimes I think I have myself some of her tastes. I like what are called Bohemians, and fellows of that sort. I have seen all sorts of society —dukes and duchesses, lords and ladies, authors and actors and painters—and, taken altogether, I think I like painters the best, and 'Bohemians' generally. They are more natural and unconventional ; they wear their hair on their shoulders if they wish, and dress picturesquely and carelessly. You see how I made *Becky* prefer them, and that sort of life, to all the fine society she moved in. Perhaps you remember where she comes down in the world, toward the end of the book, and associates with people of all sorts, Bohemians and the rest, in their garrets."

" I remember very well."

" I like that part of the book. I think that part is well done."

" As you speak of Becky Sharp, Mr. Thackeray," I said, " there is one mystery about her which I should like to have cleared up."

" What is that ? "

' Nearly at the end of the book there is a picture of Jo Sedley in his night-dress, seated—a sick old man—in his chamber ; and behind the curtain is Becky, glaring and ghastly, grasping a dagger."

"I remember."

"Beneath the picture is the single word 'Clytemnestra.'"

"Yes."

"Did Becky kill him, Mr. Thackeray?"

This question seemed to afford the person to whom it was addressed, material for profound reflection. He smoked meditatively, appeared to be engaged in endeavoring to arrive at the solution of some problem, and then with a secretive expression —a "slow smile" dawning on his face—replied:

"I don't know!"

A desultory conversation ensued on the subject of Becky Sharp, for whom, in spite of her depravity, it seemed very plain that Mr. Thackeray had a secret liking, or, if not precisely a liking, at least an amused sympathy, due to the pluck and perseverance with which she pursued the objects she had in view. And then, from this lady and her sayings and doings, the conversation passed to Mr. Thackeray's other *mauvais sujets*, male and female; and I said that I considered the old Earl of Crabs, in the sketches relating to "Mr. Deuceace," as the most finished and altogether perfect scoundrel of the whole list. To this Mr. Thackeray was disposed to assent, and I asked if the Earl was drawn from any particular person.

"I really don't know," was the reply. "I don't remember ever meeting with any special person as the original."

"Then you must have drawn him from your imagination, or from general observation."

"I suppose so—I don't know—I may have seen him somewhere."

And after smoking for several moments, with that air of silent meditation which his friends must often have observed, Mr. Thackeray added, in the tone of a man indulging in soliloquy:

"I really don't know where I get all these rascals in my books. I have certainly never *lived* with such people."

It did not seem to occur to this profound and subtle observer of human nature that daily association with the class to which the Earl of Crabs, Lord Steyne, and others belonged, was not necessary to the just delineation of the personages. He had looked from behind his glasses, with those keen eyes of his, upon the moving throng of rascaldom, in London, at Rome, on the Parisian boulevards, and everywhere, and the penetrating glance had photographed the figures upon his brain—their inward being as well as their outward show,—after which to reproduce them in his books was, so to say, a mere mechanical process.

Mr. Thackeray spoke of himself and his writings with entire candor and unreserve, of which I shall give an instance before concluding this brief sketch; and his opinions upon other writers were equally frank and outspoken. The elder Dumas, the author of "Monte Cristo" and the "Mousquetaire" stories, seemed to be an especial favorite with him.

"Dumas is charming!" he exclaimed; "every thing he writes interests me. I have been reading his 'Mémoires.' I have read fourteen of the small volumes, all that are published, and they are delightful. Dumas is a wonderful man—wonderful. He is better than Walter Scott."

"You refer, I suppose, to his historical novels, the 'Mousquetaires,' and the rest?"

"Yes. I came near writing a book on the same subject, and taking Monsieur d'Artagnan for my hero, as Dumas has done in his 'Trois Mousquetaires.' D'Artagnan was a real character of the age of Louis XIV., and wrote his own 'Mémoires.' I remember picking up a dingy little copy of them on an old bookstall in London, price sixpence, and intended to make something of it. But Dumas got ahead of me—he snaps up every thing. He is wonderful!"

"I am glad you like him, as he was always a great favorite of my own," I said; "his *verve* is unflagging."

"Yes; his good spirits seem never to change. He amuses you, and keeps you in a good humor, which is not the effect produced on me by many writers. Some books please me and enliven me, and others depress me. I never could read 'Don Quixote' with pleasure. The book makes me sad."

Further allusion to the old knight of La Mancha indicated that the source of this sadness was a profound sympathy with the crazed gentleman,—a commiseration so deep for his troubles and chimeras of the brain, that the wit and farcical humor of Sancho were insufficient, in his opinion, to relieve the shadows of the picture.

Passing from these literary discussions, Mr. Thackeray spoke of his tour in America, and said how much gratified he had been by his reception. Richmond was an attractive place to him, he declared—he had been received with the utmost kindness and attention,—and he had always looked upon the Virginians as resembling more closely his own people in England than the Americans of other States. They seemed "more homely," I think was his phrase—which I recall, from the curious employment of the word "homely" in the sense of "home-like."

"Your American travels will no doubt give you the material for a volume on this country," I said.

"Yes; I have seen a great deal," was his reply.

"Well, I don't think you will abuse us, Mr. Thackeray."

"I shall not write any thing upon America," he said; "my secretary may—he is quite capable. And, as to abusing you, if I do, I 'm ——!"

The sentence terminated in a manner rather more emphatic than would have suited the atmosphere of a drawing-room; and it was plainly to be seen that Mr. Thackeray had thoroughly made up his mind not to follow in the footsteps of Mr. Dickens, and criticise his entertainers—"throw their plates at their heads," as Scott said when he declined accepting an invitation to dine with the old Count Barras, near Paris, of whom he declared he would probably have some harsh things to say in his "Life of Napoleon." Mr. Thackeray had the instinct that, one would think, should control all persons of good feeling and good breeding, and never wrote a line, that I am aware of, which any citizen of the country, North or South, would have wished unwritten.

Further conversation upon Virginia, the character of the country, people, etc., led Mr. Thackeray to speak of what was then a mere literary intention —the composition of "The Virginians," which was not written, I think, or at least did not appear, until two or three years afterward.

"I shall write a novel with the scene laid here," he said.

"In America? I am very glad, and I hope you will be able to do so soon."

"No. I shall not write it for about two years."

"Two years?"

"Yes. It will take me at least two years to collect my materials and become acquainted with the subject. I can't write upon a subject I know nothing of. I am obliged to read up upon it, and get my ideas."

"Your work will be a novel?"

"Yes, and relating to your State. I shall give it the title of 'The Two Virginians,'"—a title which, as the reader knows, was afterward changed for the shorter and simpler "The Virginians."

As I expressed a natural pleasure at the prospect of having a novel painting Virginia life and society from the author of "Esmond," Mr. Thackeray spoke more particularly of his design, thereby exhibiting, I thought, and think still, a remarkable instance of the simplicity, directness, and absence of *secretiveness* in his character. I was nearly an entire stranger, but he spoke without reserve of his intended book, telling me his whole idea.

"I shall lay the scene in Virginia, during the Revolution," he said. "There will be two brothers, who will be prominent characters; one will take the English side in the war, and the other the American, and they will both be in love with the same girl."

"That will be an excellent plot," I said, "and your novel will be a full-blooded historical one."

"It will deal with the history of the time."

"You have a striking *dénoûment*—"

"A *dénoûment?*"

"Yorktown."

Having so said, I became suddenly aware that I had committed something closely resembling a social *faux pas*, inasmuch as I had quietly recommended to an English gentleman to take the surrender of Lord Cornwallis as the climax of his drama,

"I really must beg your pardon, Mr. Thackeray," I said with some embarrassment.

"Beg my pardon?" he said, turning his head and looking at me with a good deal of surprise.

"For my ill-breeding."

His expression of surprise was more pronounced than before at these words, and he evidently did not understand my meaning in the least.

"I mean," I said, "that I quite lost sight of the fact that I was talking with an English gentleman. Yorktown was the scene of Lord Cornwallis' surrender, and might not be an agreeable *dénoûment*."

"Ah!" he said, smiling, "it is nothing. I accept Yorktown."

"I know you admire Washington."

"Yes, indeed. He was one of the greatest men that ever lived."

My host had evidently no susceptibilities to wound in reference to these old historical matters, so I said, smiling:

"Everybody respects and loves Washington now; but is it not singular how the *result* changes our point of view? The English view in '76 was that Washington was a rebel, and if you had caught him you would probably have hanged him."

To this Mr. Thackeray replied in a tone of great earnestness:

"We had better have lost North America."

A curious episode in Thackeray's life is that which connects him with Charlotte Brontë. The author of "Jane Eyre" had long worshipped Thackeray from a distance, and had dedicated that book to him in words of the heartiest and most respectful admiration. But she had never seen him until the time of her second visit to London, when he called upon her. She afterward told Mrs. Gaskell, in describing this first call, that she found it difficult to decide whether he was speaking in jest or in earnest, and that she had, she believed, completely misunderstood an inquiry of his, made on the gentlemen's coming into the drawing-room. He asked her "if she had perceived the secret of their cigars"; to which she replied literally, discovering, a minute afterward, by the smile on several faces, that he was alluding to a passage in "Jane Eyre." Altogether, she says in one of her letters, she was "fearfully stupid," although she had felt sufficiently at her ease with the other distinguished people she had met in London. But then Thackeray, she explains, "is a Titan of mind. His presence and powers impress one deeply in an intellectual sense; I do not see him and know him as a man. All the others are subordinate." About a week later she writes as follows: " Mr. Thackeray made a morning call and sat above two hours. Mr. Smith only was in the room the whole time. He described it afterward as 'a queer scene,' and I suppose it was. The giant sat before me; I was moved to speak of some of his shortcomings (literary of course): one by one the faults came into my head, and one by one I brought them out, and sought some explanation or defence. He did defend himself, like a great Turk and heathen; that is to say, the excuses were often worse than the crime itself. The matter ended in decent amity; if all be well, I am to dine at his house this evening." She attended one of his lectures, which, she says, was a genuine treat to her. "It was given in Willis' Rooms, where the Almack balls are held—a great painted and gilded saloon, with long sofas for benches. The audience was said to be the cream of London society, and it looked so I did not at all expect the great lecturer would know me or notice me under these circumstances, with admiring duchesses and countesses seated in rows before him; but he met me as I entered, shook hands, took me to his mother, whom I had not seen before, and introduced me. She is a fine, handsome, young-looking old lady; was very gracious, and called, with one of her grand-daughters, next day." The lady who accompanied Miss Brontë noticed, after they had taken their seats, that Thackeray was pointing out her companion to several of his friends, but she hoped Miss Brontë herself would not perceive it. After some time, however, during which many heads had been turned round, and many glasses put up, in order to look at the author of "Jane Eyre," Miss Brontë said: "I am afraid Mr. Thackeray has been playing me a trick"; but she soon became too much absorbed in the lecture to notice the attention that was being paid. When the lecture was ended, Thackeray came down from the platform, and making his way toward her, asked her for her opinion, "a question eminently characteristic, and reminding me, even in this his moment of triumph, of that inquisitive restlessness, that absence of what I considered desirable self-control, which were amongst his faults. He should not have cared, just then, to ask what I thought, or what anybody thought; but he *did* care, and he was too natural to conceal, too impulsive to repress his wish. Well! if I blamed his over-eagerness, I liked his naïveté. I would have praised him; I had plenty of praise in my heart, but alas! no words on my lips. Who *has* words at the right moment? I stammered some lame expressions, but was truly glad when other people, coming up with profuse congratulations, covered up my deficiency by their redundancy." This last paragraph, to say truth, is not copied from Miss Brontë's letters on Thackeray, but from Miss Snow's comments in "Villette," upon a similar action on the part of M. Paul Emanuel, —comments that Mrs. Gaskell, when she came to read them, at once recognized as being "almost identical" with the remarks that Lucy Snow's creator had made concerning Thackeray when she related this incident to her. Miss Brontë was not equally gratified by all the lectures; that on Fielding deeply distressed her, on account of what she considered its levity of tone. "The hour spent in listening to it," she says, "was a painful hour. Had Thackeray owned a son, grown or growing, and a son brilliant but reckless, would he have spoken in that light way of courses that lead to disgrace and the grave?" It was poor Branwell Brontë, doubtless, she was thinking of, when she penned those lines.

# CHAPTER XVII.

### SOME YOUNGER WRITERS.

Anecdotes and Reminiscences of William Black, Matthew Arnold, William Morris, Jean Ingelow, Owen Meredith, "Ouida."

IN this chapter are grouped together a number of newspaper cuttings in regard to some of the celebrities among the present generation of authors. The embarrassment of riches, however, which occurs with most of the elder writers, who have been much interviewed and written about, gives way, in the case of the younger ones, to a poverty of details that renders even trifles of importance. Some of the paragraphs here collected are consequently given to the reader with the full knowledge that their interest mainly depends upon the dearth of fuller and more authentic information.

**WILLIAM BLACK.**

These two newspaper cuttings in regard to

the leader among the younger novelists of the day may be of interest to his admirers.

Among very pleasant English recollections of a year ago comes an evening spent at the house of a writer as well known on this side of the water as in his own land.

It was a reception given late in the season, but the hospitable drawing-rooms were filled. The host and hostess entertained with that charming ease and pleasant cordiality which is so notably English, and if unlike our hearty American warmth, answers the purpose equally well.

It afforded us a curious pleasure to watch the arrivals and note the announcements. There were many faces to be remembered, many names whose familiar power deepened when we stood face to face with their owners. Presently through the crowd came a young man of twenty-eight or thirty—slightly built, with earnest eyes and a long brown mustache. There was nothing of the conventional literary man in his appearance. His dress was a faultless evening attire. He wore the fresh *boutonnière* so indispensable from ten o'clock on Piccadilly to midnight in a Hyde-Park drawing-room. He carried himself with a careless ease which had in it neither affectation nor consciousness that a hundred eyes were watching him, that many voices had said half audibly, "There is the author of 'A Princess of Thule.'"

To us, at that time, he seemed simply the man whose genius had wrought Coquette, the gentle-hearted daughter of Heth ; and noting his youthful appearance, his quiet, unobservant manner, we looked vainly for outward indications of his peculiar power. Presently, however, when engaged in conversation, there came a new light into his face. His eyes brightened with a keen intelligence, and the deepening lines about his mouth gave a suggestion of reserve force.

Mr. Black is a charming conversationalist. He is extremely modest about his literary successes, but is willing to gratify one's curiosity about the whys and wherefores of some of his stories in the most agreeable way. I remember when some one, with true Yankee inquisitiveness, said, " Oh, Mr. Black, why did *Coquette* die ? " he answered with a mixture of modesty and good-will, pleasant to recall : " Why, you see, I did n't want to make her die—but I had to do it. If she had lived, the reader would not have remembered her six hours after he had closed the book ! "—*Appletons' Journal.*

Of Mr. Black individually I fear I can give only an inadequate impression, so much of his charm depends upon his personal presence. I can say that he is slight and not very tall, with a finely modelled head and face, broad forehead, and strong, rather square jaws, dark hair, and expressive dark eyes that regard you most kindly through the habitual glasses that he wears; a dark mustache; and has the faintest suspicion of a difficulty with his *r*'s; that he is courteous and genial in manner, with a little trick of looking down as he talks and suddenly raising his eyes with a quick, keen expression at any remark that interests or amuses him. In conversation he is charming, and in his own house and at his own table a most gracious and kindly host. His fund of story, anecdote, and repartee is inexhaustible, while to be with him is but constantly to recall Dick Steele's tribute to the Lady Elizabeth Hastings, that " to know her was a liberal education." He has slender and well-formed hands, and he is always a *preux chevalier* in his appearance. This is only a bald description of him, but more is impossible; it is necessary to see him and hear him to thoroughly appreciate his varied attributes. Mrs. Black is, as according to the law of contrasts she should be, a blonde with blue eyes, a fair complexion, and soft plenteous golden hair that waves about her head most artistically. She is clever and interesting beyond most women, all the more so perhaps because of the little air of sadness that surrounds her. She has a sweet voice and pleasant manners, is an intense admirer of her husband, though thoroughly capable of criticising keenly and impartially his work, only desirous that he shall not lose his position with the public that he has so honestly won.—*The Home Journal.*

## MATTHEW ARNOLD.

Mr. Arnold is a man of so much prominence in the world of letters, that it is only because of the poverty of details in regard to his personality that we have, as it were, relegated him into a corner.

In appearance the apostle of culture is, if not actually disappointing, at least very different from the ideal one might form of him from his writings. He is a large man, with prominent and somewhat harsh features, who parts his hair in the middle, and wears very ill-fitting clothes. His face indicates character and force more than refinement, and altogether he gives the impression of a cynical and disappointed man of the world rather than of a poet. His manners are cold and distant, even to haughtiness—Mallock, who has caricatured him in his "New Republic" under the name of Mr. Luke, calls him "supercilious-looking"—and he is not generally liked. By his few intimates, however, he is fully appreciated. Doubtless the coldness is only exterior—the incrustation behind which a sensitive nature protects itself from the indifference of the world. That he is really a man of warm sensibilities is well known to his friends. Within the limit of his means he is one of the most generous of men, and many stories might be told of his unostentatious private charities. "That Mr. Arnold is not an idealist only," says a writer in the *University Magazine*, " but as kindly-natured in matters practical as he is amusing in companionship or sparkling in criticism, we have had occasion to know. An artisan poet with a true lyric gift, delicate health, and a wife and family to keep, told us how once, not long ago, when things were so bad with him that his children were asking for bread, Matthew Arnold sent such timely and generous supplies as brought grateful tears to the eyes of the recipients, and, interesting himself in their case, got a subscription started for the poor fellow ; all was so delicately done that the mention of Matthew Arnold's name brings out a sincere 'God bless him' in that family."

### WILLIAM MORRIS

is described as entirely free from the peculiarities which are usually thought to appertain to literary men. Like R. D. Blackmore, who at first sight looks more like a farmer than a poet or a novelist, yet who grows upon the mind by the depth of his eye and the force of his presence, Mr. Morris might pass along in his easy, unconventional costume without attracting the attention of his worshippers—unless, indeed, they were to scan the facial contour with an artist's eye. He is physically strong and hearty enough to afford good ground for the hope that he may live many years to enjoy the honors showered upon him. Mr. Morris' country-place, at which he resides during the greater portion of the year, is a mediæval building, with fine grounds around it where he can enjoy to the fullest extent those rural solitudes that are the delight of all poets. Mr. Morris is an artist also, and has produced excellent studies in distemper. He is, further, a thorough man of business and the managing head of the house of Morris, Marshall, Faulkner, & Co., a great emporium and laboratory for the production of artistic fabrics of the most varied, costly, and beautiful description. The house was founded by Morris in 1861, in conjunction with his artist friends, Madox Brown, Burne Jones, Rossetti, and Webb. Having little capital to commence with, it was conducted on a small scale at first. Nor was it successful at once. The outside world was inclined to look upon it as merely the enterprise of a few young dreamers. The production of ornamental furniture and stained-glass windows was the principal work undertaken at first, Morris acting as designer, as well as his friends. Little by little the beauty of the new designs began to impress the public. As business improved, new departments were started. Carpets and paper-hangings were added to the list of wares, Morris himself working out the patterns to the smallest details; and the house is at present one of the largest and wealthiest establishments in London.

### JEAN INGELOW.

From the pages of an English periodical called *The Queen*, I extract the following account of an interview with this charming poetess, written by Miss L. M. Alcott.

"Will you come and call on Jean Ingelow?" said my hostess, one fine day. Of course I would. So away we went along a shady lane, with the old oaks of Holland Park on the one side, and the ivy-crowned walls of Aubury House on the other; for, though a part of London, Notting Hill is rich in gardens, lawns, and parks, such as one sees only in England. Coming at last to a quiet street, where all the houses were gay with window-boxes full of flowers, we reached Miss Ingelow's. In the drawing-room we found the mother of the poetess, a truly beautiful old lady, in widow's cap and gown, with the sweetest, serenest face I ever saw. Two daughters sat with her, both older than I had fancied them to be, but both very attractive women. Eliza looked as if she wrote the poetry, Jean the prose—the former wore curls, had a delicate face, fine eyes, and that indescribable something which suggests genius; the latter was plain, rather stout, hair touched with gray, shy yet cordial manners, and a clear, straightforward glance, which I liked so much that I forgave her on the spot for writing those dull stories. Gerald Massey was with them, a dapper little man, with a large, tall head, and very un-English manner. Being oppressed with "the mountainous me," he rather bored the company with "my poems, my plans, and my publishers," till Miss Eliza politely devoted herself to him, leaving my friend to chat with the lovely old lady, and myself with Jean. Both being bashful, and both laboring under the delusion that it was proper to allude to each other's works, we tried to exchange a few compliments, blushed, hesitated, laughed, and wisely took refuge in a safer subject. Jean had been abroad, so we pleasantly compared notes, and I enjoyed the sound of a peculiarly musical voice, in which I seemed to hear the breezy rhythm of some of her charming songs. The ice which surrounds every Englishman and woman was beginning to melt, when Massey disturbed me to ask what was thought of his books in America.

As I really had not the remotest idea, I said so; whereat he looked blank, and fell upon Longfellow, who seems to be the only one of our poets whom the English know or care about. The conversation became general, and soon after it was necessary to leave, lest the safety of the nation should be endangered by overstepping the fixed limits of a morning call. Later, I learned that Miss Ingelow was extremely conservative, and was very indignant when a petition for woman's right to vote was offered for her signature. A rampant Radical told me this, and shook her handsome head pathetically over Jean's narrowness; but when I heard that once a week several poor souls dined comfortably in the pleasant home of the poetess, I forgave her conservatism, and regretted that an unconquerable aversion to dinner parties made me decline her invitation.

### OWEN MEREDITH.

Of Robert Bulwer, the present Earl Lytton, a writer in *Lippincott's Magazine* who was conducted over the Lytton mansion at Knebworth by the poet himself, presents the following description: "It would be difficult to find a better example of the extreme unaffectedness of modern Englishmen than 'Owen Meredith.' He speaks in a pure accent, without any 'throatiness' or drawl, and his manner has a charming simplicity and urbanity. A very brief acquaintance with him is sufficient to show that he has the discretion of the diplomat, the sympathetic delicacy of the poet, the catholicity of the man of the world, and the ease and dignity of the man of society. A quiet humorousness, occasionally edged with a touch of satire and cynicism, characterizes his conversation ; but he is a man of deep and sincere feelings, which are sometimes expressed with an amusing bluntness of epithet. When showing us through one of the principal apartments, he pointed to a picture: ' There is that brute Rousseau. There was also a picture of Robespierre,' he added; 'but I could n't stand that, and I had it taken away.' In personal appearance he bears a marked resemblance to the pictures of his father,—the same long face, dark-complexioned, with sad-looking eyes, a full straight beard, and a prominent aquiline nose. He is firmly built, but rather below than above medium height, and not of a massive frame. That he is nearly fifty years of age scarcely seems credible; a reasonable guess would put his age at about forty."

OUIDA.

Miss Louisa de la Ramé, the flashy genius

who writes under the name of Ouida, is a lady on the shady side of forty, and is thus described by a newspaper correspondent: "She is a fine-looking and very stylish person, not handsome, but decidedly striking in appearance, and the only well-dressed Englishwoman I have as yet seen; her toilettes being very elegant and tasteful, though she somewhat mars their effect by letting her back hair flow loose over her shoulders. Her hair is abundant and of a tawny yellow in color." "Her manners are fascinating," says another authority; "her conversation lively; her eyes bright and expressive. She is saucy and audacious in her remarks, and sometimes indulges in ladylike slang; but in spite of all this she is a great favorite among English and American residents at Florence, and they are glad to accept invitations to her villa, for she entertains magnificently." She is said, however, to have a great dislike to her own sex, and rarely admits ladies to her receptions, confining her invitations to the masculine notabilities who happen to be visiting Florence. But her choicest affections are reserved for her dogs, whereof she has a large number, who fill up her house and surround her wherever she goes. She says they are more faithful than the human race.

Whenever one of them dies, he or she is buried with more respect than is sometimes shown to men and women. A story is told about one of her countrymen, who recently called on "Ouida" by permission, and showed much pride at being allowed to pay his respects in person to so famous a literary woman. He returned to the hotel at which he was staying not altogether charmed with his visit. "Well, what did you do at 'Ouida's'?" queried one of his lady friends. "I fed her dog with buns." "And what did she say? What did she do?" "Nothing; she fed the dog too." "Ouida" is fond of driving, and she is often seen in the Cascine and along the Lung' Arno, in a lofty and stylish drag, holding the reins herself and driving with such haste that she runs into hay-wagons.

**THE END.**

www.ingramcontent.com/pod-product-compliance
Lightning Source LLC
Chambersburg PA
CBHW020242240426
43672CB00006B/615